Teaching
PHYSICAL EDUCATION

Teaching
PHYSICAL EDUCATION

A **Handbook**
FOR PRIMARY & SECONDARY SCHOOL TEACHERS

Richard BAILEY

Routledge
Taylor & Francis Group

LONDON AND NEW YORK

To Rob and Mikaela Bailey
My Brother and New Sister
With Love

First published in Great Britain and the United States by Routledge Limited in 2001
Reprinted in 2003
Reprinted in 2005, 2006, 2007 by Routledge

2 Park Square,   270 Madison Ave,
Milton Park,   New York
Abingdon, Oxon,   NY 10016
OX14 4RN

Transferred to Digital Printing 2010

www.routledge.com

British Library Cataloguing in Publication Data

A CIP record for this book is available from the British Library.

ISBN 10: 0 7494 3446 5
ISBN 13: 9780 7494 3446 5

Typeset by Saxon Graphics Ltd, Derby

Publisher's Note
The publisher has gone to great lengths to ensure the quality of this reprint but points out that some imperfections in the original may be apparent.

Contents

Series Editor's foreword

Physical education has again become an area of great debate at both government and school level. With increased interest in health and physical education, this book is timely and appropriate for teachers across phases. Physical education has its place within the National Curriculum, but frequently it does not get the attention it requires within a curriculum. Teaching and understanding the physical education curriculum requires a breadth of knowledge in a variety of physical education areas, as well as being a specialist in one area. Teachers entering the world of physical education need to appreciate the complexities of teaching physical education as well as understanding that the pupils they will teach will have a broad spectrum of ability and awareness of health and fitness issues. Developing a physical education teacher requires an acknowledgement of theses issues. This book aims to help teachers in this role by giving authoritative guidance and practical tasks, backed up by extensive theoretical perspectives for engaging with ideas and concepts of physical education across the curriculum.

Teaching Physical Education has been included in the Kogan Page Teaching Series because physical education has an important role to play within the National Curriculum, and thus will affect every pupil to the age of 16.

Richard Bailey has assembled a rich source that reveals an awareness of the broad academic, social, political and cultural contexts in which the challenges of teaching and learning about physical education are addressed. The chapters draw widely from leading experts in the field and reflect both pragmatic and theoretical issues that are of relevance to the delivery on the science National Curriculum. All chapters have a commitment to providing a high-quality learning experience. They reflect not only on the teaching of the subject area itself, but also on the learning outcomes from engaging with the variety of concepts and issues related to teaching physical education as a subject within the National Curriculum.

The key elements of this book are its combination of generic and specific teaching ideas, theoretical perspectives and vision for future developments. These significant elements are presented to help experienced and newly qualified teachers alike. By addressing issues across phases, this book will be uniquely helpful for all teaching professionals.

Professor Gill Nicholls
King's College
University of London

Foreword

Physical education, both as a field of study and as a preparation for teachers, seems to have gone through several phases since I was a student. Then, physical education was struggling to find respectability as a field of study, having moved from an almost completely practical approach to becoming, for the first time in the United Kingdom, an academic 'subject' worthy of degree (BEd) status. The syllabi produced for those first BEd fourth year courses can most kindly be described as eclectic. They depended heavily on applications from a range of other subjects and fields of study, with perhaps the most developed being the early psychology of motor skill. It was a long time before physical education as a field of study emerged in its own right. For the past 30 years of the last century, physical education continued to depend on aspects of sports science, often over-theorized and under-applied to the everyday experiences of physical education.

This book represents for me the 'coming of age' of physical education as an area of study for prospective teachers. Richard Bailey has successfully used his insights from researching a range of disciplines and from proven good practice to draw together a synthesis of knowledge, theory and practice, which will provide a wealth of resources for students and serving teachers of physical education. Currently, all over the world, leaders of physical education are fighting to retain or secure sufficient time in school curricula for their subject. It is therefore particularly important that all teachers are able to articulate clearly and with belief what physical education is, along with its distinctive contribution to the development of children and young people. It is also crucial that teachers are able to nurture their own beliefs in physical education by intelligent reflection and continual questioning, reconstruction and reaffirmation. In the United Kingdom, a new national sports strategy is being implemented, which identifies and depends on physical education and school sport as the foundation for all sports development. It is even more important in this context that teachers are able to discriminate the distinctive in physical education rather than be beguiled into mere sports education.

FOREWORD

This book provides a framework for student teachers and experienced teachers to achieve rather than only aspire towards the ideal of becoming 'reflective practitioners' ie hands-on, active teachers with minds fully engaged with the processes of learning that they are trying to stimulate and support. The format encourages active participation in systematic analysis by both individual readers and groups. The examples of good practice further affirm the joy and belief in physical education that brought most of us into the subject, and even more importantly, keep us engaged and energized by it.

Margaret Talbot
Chief Executive
Central Council of Physical Recreation

Preface

There are few subjects as important for children's development and general education as physical education. As is explained in this book, the contribution that physical education can make is both distinctive and significant. Many pupils come to lessons with enthusiasm and great expectations. To meet this challenge, and to make the most of the great opportunities that physical education offers, inexperienced teachers need guidance and advice to extend their knowledge of the subject and their awareness of the principles of good, safe practice.

Teaching Physical Education aims to provide a comprehensive guide for teachers of physical education at both primary and secondary schools. The book focuses on the fundamental skills of teaching, particularly the skills that underpin the planning, delivery and assessment in lessons, but it also offers guidance on aspects of physical education teaching that have been stressed more recently by policy makers, such as the use of information and communication technology, and citizenship education.

Three groups make up the main audience. I hope that trainee teachers will find *Teaching Physical Education* a useful guide to the skills, knowledge and understanding needed to meet the subject-specific requirements for the achievement of Qualified Teacher Status. It offers advice on meeting new classes, establishing a positive, controlled class environment and the fundamental teaching skills needed during school experience. Newly qualified teachers should be able to draw upon the practical suggestions, background information and guidance on good practice to support themselves through their early years in the teaching profession. I would also hope that school mentors and higher education tutors will find the book a valuable source of sensible guidance, useful tasks and ideas for professional development that can be used to support their work with inexperienced colleagues.

The content and structure of the book

In writing *Teaching Physical Education*, I attempted to meet two needs. On the one hand, inexperienced teachers of physical education need simple, accessible and practical advice on teaching the subject. On the other hand, they also need to be aware of some of the theoretical underpinnings of good practice in physical education teaching. Therefore, each of the chapters offers some background to the topics discussed, including reference to relevant research findings, and proceeds to explain the essential skills and knowledge in the area. Each chapter also includes a series of practical tasks, which can extend the reader's understanding of the topic, as well as offer him or her an opportunity to apply certain principles to specific situations. Chapters conclude with brief summaries of the content, as well as suggested further reading.

I hope you find this a useful source of guidance and information.

Acknowledgements

I would like to take this opportunity to offer my great thanks for support and encouragement to friends, colleagues and students at Canterbury Christ Church University College, Reading University and Leeds Metropolitan University. I would particularly like to acknowledge my debt to Tony Macfadyen and Mike Osborne, both lecturers in physical education at Reading. Much of the philosophy that lies behind the ideas presented in this book originates from an extremely challenging and exciting time working alongside Tony and Mike. I am very grateful to have been given the chance to work with them both.

1 The physical education curriculum

Introduction

This chapter examines the scope and content of physical education in schools. It is important for trainee and newly qualified teachers to be aware of different interpretations of their subject, and to consider their own views. As professionals, physical educators need to develop their own philosophy of teaching, one that guides their practice and the character of their daily encounters with pupils. They also need to be critically aware of policy documentation and guidance from central agencies.

Objectives

By the end of this chapter you should:

- understand the importance of physical education, physical activity and movement for all pupils;
- be familiar with various interpretations of the aims and purposes of physical education;
- know the statutory requirements related to the content of physical education.

Children and movement

'Physical education makes me feel as if I could fly away!' (11-year-old from Leeds, England, quoted in Talbot, 1999).

There is little doubting the central importance of movement and physical activity in the lives of children and young people. Consider the following recent research findings (see Bailey, 1999a and 1999b):

- Physical activity play is the first appearing and most frequently occurring expression of play in infants.
- Children in all cultures around the world engage in both spontaneous and rule-governed forms of physical activity.
- Most children would rather take part in physical activities than in any other endeavour.
- They would prefer to succeed in these activities than in classroom-based work.
- Physical competence is a major factor influencing social acceptance in children of all ages and both sexes.
- Regular physical activity can make significant positive contributions to physical, mental and emotional well-being in children.

Bailey (1999b) coined the phrase *infans ludens* (child the player) to draw attention to the essentially active, playful nature of children's lives. Similarly, Bruner (1983: 121) suggests that activity, play and movement constitute the 'culture of childhood', and this idea has been extended by Bjorkvold (1989), who argues that any education that disregards such experiences creates a harmful and dispiriting tension. He expresses this view as a clash between 'child culture' and 'school culture':

Child Culture	School Culture
play	study
being in	reading about
physical proximity	physical distance
testing one's own limits	respecting boundaries set by others
the unexpected	the expected
sensory	intellectual
physical movement	physical inactivity
I move and I learn!	Sit still!

It may not be surprising that both teachers and pupils regularly rate physical education lessons among the most important curriculum areas (Birtwistle and Brodie, 1991). Pupils also regularly vote it among the most popular subjects. This reaction to the subject offers physical education teachers a great advantage, as most pupils come to them highly motivated and eager to learn. It also places a responsibility on those teachers not to turn the pupils off physical education and even physical activity, as can sometimes happen.

Task 1.1

Spend a few moments listing your personal experiences of physical activity and physical education. Not all of these experiences need be positive, and it is important to include negative feelings and memories, as well. Talk to friends and colleagues about their experiences. Are there any emerging themes and patterns? Which are the most frequently reported experiences? Are there significant differences between the reports of physical education professionals and those outside the subject? Are there any differences between males' and females' responses? What sorts of experiences of physical education and physical activity have people found off-putting?

Some of the most useful people to whom trainee or newly qualified teachers can talk are those who hated their subject at school. Predictably, most physical education teachers loved the subject as pupils, and sometimes find it difficult to appreciate contrary experiences. However, coming to understand such experiences can make them more sensitive when dealing with their pupils, and may help them avoid some of the behaviours that have put some people off physical education and physical activity in the past.

Aims and purposes of physical education

'Cheshire Puss,' she began, rather timidly… 'Would you tell me, please, which way I ought to go from here?' 'That depends a good deal on where you want to get to,' said the Cat. 'I don't much care where,' said Alice. 'Then it doesn't matter which way you go,' said the Cat. 'So long as I get somewhere,' Alice added as an explanation. 'Oh, you're sure to do that,' said the Cat, 'if you only walk long enough.'
(Lewis Carroll, *Alice's Adventures in Wonderland*)

As the above quotation from *Alice in Wonderland* makes clear, it is very difficult to know which way to proceed without an understanding of where you want to end up. Aims give a sense of direction and purpose. The physical education teacher, today, has to address and prioritize a host of aims, including aims deriving from statutory regulations (like the National Curriculum) and from school policy. The teacher, as a professional, also needs to reflect on his or her own views of the subject, and the aims they express.

Task 1.2

What are the aims of physical education? What do *you* think are the purposes of the subject?

For 10 minutes, brainstorm your initial ideas. Then highlight the ones that you feel are especially central to the subject, and rank them in order of importance.

Repeat this task from time to time throughout the year. Does your list change? Do you add or remove items? Does your ordering of the central aims change?

Numerous authors have offered their own views on the aims of physical education. Talbot (1999), for example, claims that the subject 'aims to develop physical literacy and integrated development of the whole person', whilst Almond (2000: 12) proposes (among other things) 'moving beyond play into disciplined forms of physical activity such as sport and dance', and Parry (1998: 64) talks of 'the development of certain human excellences of a valued kind'. The National Curriculum for England and Wales also has its list of aims and purposes, which are outlined below:

PE offers opportunities for children to:

- become skilful and intelligent performers;
- acquire and develop skills, performing with increasing physical competence and confidence, in a range of physical activities and contexts;
- learn how to select and apply skills, tactics and compositional ideas to suit activities that need different approaches and ways of thinking;
- develop their ideas in a creative way;
- set targets for themselves and compete against others, individually and as team members;
- understand what it takes to persevere, succeed and acknowledge others' success;
- respond to a variety of challenges in a range of physical contexts and environments;
- take the initiative, lead activity and focus on improving aspects of their own performance;
- discover their own aptitudes and preferences for different activities;

- make informed decisions about the importance of exercise in their lives;
- develop positive attitudes to participation in physical activity.

(http://www.standards.dfee.gov.uk/schemes/phe/peks12/aims/)

One message that should come across from these different presentations of the aims and purposes of physical education is that the subject has a distinctive and significant contribution to make to the overall education of every pupil. Moreover, 'if the potential and range of the physical education experience is not fully realized, then that child cannot be said to be properly educated' (Bailey, 1999a: 34). The following section considers the scope and possibilities of physical education.

Dimensions of physical education

There are many different ways of thinking about the content and character of physical education (see, for example, the different contributions to Armstrong, 1990, 1992, 1996, and Almond, 1997). A useful framework for understanding the subject is provided by Arnold (1979; adapted by Bailey, 1999b):

- education *about* movement;
- education *through* movement;
- education *in* movement.

Education about movement

This aspect stresses the value of introducing pupils to a range of physical activities, as well as the concepts, rules and procedures associated with them. Of course, there are many activities that pupils might experience, and each can make a contribution to their development and education.

The National Curriculum (DfEE, 2000) sets out the activity areas that pupils should experience, and the expected standards of pupils' performance (the attainment target). The activity areas are:

- dance activities;
- games activities;
- gymnastics activities;
- swimming activities and water safety;
- athletic activities;
- outdoor and adventurous activities.

The knowledge, skills and understanding in the Programmes of Study (PoS) identify the aspects of physical education in which pupils make progress:

- acquiring and developing skills;
- selecting and applying skills, tactics and compositional ideas;
- evaluating and improving;
- knowledge and understanding of fitness and health.

These themes can be realized through each activity area, and there is detailed guidance in the National Curriculum support material in how they can be developed from 5 years to 16 years (see http://www.nc.uk.net and http://standards.dfee.gov.uk; see also Chapters 2 and 8 of this book).

Table 1.1 summarizes the different activity areas through which pupils at different stages of their schooling should be taught knowledge, skills and understanding of physical education.

Table 1.1 Activity areas through which knowledge, skills and understanding should be taught

Key Stage	Age of Pupils	Activity Areas
1	5–7	dance games gymnastics
2	7–11	dance games gymnastics
		and *two* from: swimming and water safety athletic activities outdoor and adventurous activities
3	11–14	games
		and *three* from (including at least one of dance and gym): dance gymnastics swimming and water safety athletic activities outdoor and adventurous activities
4	14–16	*two* from: games dance gymnastics swimming and water safety athletic activities outdoor and adventurous activities

In learning *about* movement, it is important that children come to know the range and character of the activity areas. Performance of these activities constitutes a vital aspect of this knowledge. By taking part in different structured activities, pupils can come to know *how* to move in particular situations to achieve certain outcomes. At the same time, they also need to come to know *that* some ways of moving offer success or are more aesthetically pleasing than others. An adequate physical education encompasses both kinds of knowledge: knowing *how* and knowing *that* (Bailey, 1999b).

To constitute a physical education, rather than merely physical *training*, pupils need to think about their actions; they need to plan ahead and reflect upon their movement. A continuous cycle of planning, performing and evaluating contributes to the development both of pupils' physical skills and of their understanding of the procedures underlying these activities.

Clay (1997) cautions against viewing these processes as sedentary, or purely intellectual, operations. Planning and evaluating are not add-ons to performance in physical education: they inevitably occur at the same time as performance. Planning takes place as a pupil prepares for a gymnastics action or selects a team-mate to pass to. Pupils evaluate whenever they reflect on the outcome of a move, the success of a strike or the quality of a sequence. Of course, there may be times when the teacher thinks it is appropriate to focus on the intellectual aspects of the activity. Some pupils may find it difficult to excel in the performance of some skill, but can reveal high levels of knowledge and understanding in choreographing advance routine, or in observing and coaching others. This may particularly be the case for those for whom a severe physical disability limits their ability to perform certain actions, but is generally valuable for pupils of all abilities. One head of a secondary school physical education department made the following observation, after broadening the focus of his teaching to stress and value planning and evaluating, alongside performance: 'All of a sudden, pupils who had thought that PE wasn't for them because they couldn't perform the skills well were getting praise and being valued by peers in lessons. They started realizing that they could make their own contribution to the lesson, and that it was valuable and appreciated.'

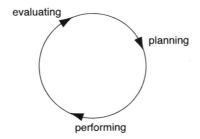

Figure 1.1 The cycle of planning, performing and evaluating

Different children enjoy and succeed in different activities, and the breadth of the physical education curriculum is a recognition of this fact. A narrow conception of competitive team-games-centred curriculum threatens to alienate a large proportion of the school population, as well as rob them of valuable learning experiences. An adequate education *about* movement, therefore, introduces the full range of movement experiences, and offers each pupil the opportunity to excel. For a recent discussion of one aspect of this theme, the reader is advised to consult the Institute of Youth Sports' report on 'Girl-friendly physical education' (2000).

Education through movement

This aspect of the physical education curriculum refers to the use of physical activities as a means of achieving educational goals that are not intrinsically part of those activities. An important aspect of this concept, and one that is particularly significant during the primary years, is the contribution physical education can make to work in other areas of the curriculum. Movement is particularly well placed to act as a medium for learning across the whole curriculum since it plays so fundamental a role in children's general learning and development: in the words of Bruner (1983), movement represents 'the culture of childhood'.

Movement experiences can create a learning environment that is enabling and fun, allowing pupils to relax and enjoy learning. By presenting learning situations as games and play, teachers can encourage pupils who may have built up resistance to lower their defences, their frustrations and anxieties, and develop their skills and understanding incidentally as they engage in physical activity. Also, as physical activity and play are universal to all children around the world, pupils become involved in experiences that bridge differences in social or cultural background or intelligence (see Bailey, 1999b, for references to research in this area).

Nowhere is the potential for education through movement more apparent than in the use of language. Hopper, Grey and Maude (2000: 91) suggest that 'translating movements into spoken language in a variety of contexts offers a treasure chest of descriptive, directional and action words for children to explore and experience'. The scope of language usage implicit within physical education is vast, and cutting across the activity areas is a language of *description, quality* and *expression*. Simply participating in physical education lessons provides an environment in which pupils are led to use language naturally and purposefully. They read instructions on work-cards, record scores and devise notation systems routines, and in each case the activity occurs in a meaningful context.

Physical education can support pupils' knowledge, skills and understanding across the whole curriculum. Table 1.2 highlights some of the areas of the curriculum, key skills and thinking skills to which physical education is expected to make a contribution (see also Chapters 9 and 10 for discussions of physical education's relationship to information technology and citizenship respectively). A few examples of applications are suggested in the table. Add your own ideas to the table, referring to the National Curriculum guidance (http://www.nc.uk.net/about/about_pe.html) if you need any clues.

Education in movement

If we believe in the value of education in physical activity for the... child then we believe that, by giving the child the experience (and skills necessary for the experience) of movement activities, we are introducing him/her to a 'physical' dimension which should be included in education for its intrinsic value and for the satisfaction which such movement experiences can bring.
(Williams, 1989: 21)

Education *in* movement is the most fundamental dimension of the physical education curriculum. Through engaging in physical activities and through exploring the possibilities and the limitations of those activities, pupils come to experience them from 'inside', rather than as disinterested observers. An important function of physical education lessons must be to inspire pupils with a love of formal and informal physical activities. To do so, teachers must realize that physical education is much more than a collection of strategies of keeping pupils fit and healthy, or useful tricks through which to teach less palatable parts of the curriculum. They are activities and experiences that are valuable and worth while *in their own right*. Of course, there are powerful extrinsic benefits to be gathered from participation in physical activities, too, but the ultimate importance of these activities lies in their intrinsic worth.

The ultimate justification of physical education rests with the distinctive natures of physical activity and movement, and their great importance to the lives of pupils. Games, dance and other forms of activity represent experiences that are valuable aspects of our culture. If pupils cannot come to see the activity from the perspective of an 'insider', they will never recognize the true appeal or beauty of that activity. If they are denied the opportunity of these experiences, their education will not be complete. These experiences are part of the process of becoming a civilized human being (Bailey, 1999b).

Table 1.2 Some contributions of physical education to learning across the curriculum

	Spiritual Development	Moral Development	Social Development	Cultural Development	Literacy	Numeracy	ICT	Thinking Skills	Work-related	Education in Sustainable Development
Dance	responses to poetry and religious themes	constructive feedback on compositions	sharing ideas in composition and appreciation	multicultural/ folk dance	responding to poems, stories and rhymes	patterns and pathways	recording notation	planning a dance in response to a range of stimuli	planning inter-school dance event	environmental themes as stimuli for dance
Games	dealing with success and failure	sensitivity to individual differences	co-operation and communication within a team	traditional games	adjectives and adverbs to describe movements	scoring and recording	recording scores, planning leagues	tactics and strategy	organizing competitions	warming up and cooling down
Gymnastics	sense of achievement through sequence planning	counter-balances	collaboration of paired sequence	cultural themes as stimuli for movement	describing the work of others	shape, direction, symmetry/ asymmetry	designing apparatus layouts using drawing packages	critically evaluating sequences	assisting teachers with gym club	importance of flexibility for healthy lifestyle
Swimming	addressing personal fears and insecurities	life-saving	personal responsibility through water safety	discussing cultural norms of body shape and body covering	writing safety rules for pool	timing, fluid dynamics	data analysis of times	coaching partners using teaching points	accompanying younger pupils to pool, and ensuring safe behaviour	swimming for health
Athletics	reflection on personal achievement	accepting authority of scorers	planning and improving relays	Olympic ideals of national pride and international co-operation	giving feedback on jumping actions	measuring, timing, data handling	recording times, distances and heights	assessing throwing techniques against criteria	planning athletics festival	relationship between different events and types of physical fitness
Outdoor and Adventurous Activities	adventure experiences	co-operating in climbing/ abseiling	communication games, taking responsibility	urban and natural environments	reaching agreement in group problem-solving	distance, use of compass, angles	devising orienteering course	co-operative problem-solving tasks	taking committee roles for outdoor pursuits club	environmental awareness

Summary

This chapter has explored different conceptions of physical education. It is vital for all teachers to articulate their own philosophy of physical education, and to let that philosophy guide their day-to-day dealings with pupils. There is no expectation that teachers will uncritically accept the positions discussed in the chapter. On the contrary, it is the duty of a professional to question received wisdom, and to reflect on his or her own experiences and values. The 'Further reading' section, below, suggests sources of ideas that may provoke further thought and reflection.

The main points to consider from this chapter are: 1) teachers need to read, discuss and reflect on the aims, justifications and philosophies of physical education that may influence their practice; 2) they should be familiar with statutory requirements and broader educational goals.

Further reading

Almond, L (1996) Physical education and primary schools, in *Teaching Physical Education 5–11*, ed R P Bailey and T M Macfadyen, Continuum, London

ICSSPE (2001) Proceedings of the World Summit on Physical Education, November 3–5, Berlin, 1999, International Council of Sport Science and Physical Education, Berlin

Laws, C and Fisher, R (1999) Pupils' interpretation of physical education, in *Learning and Teaching in Physical Education*, ed C Hardy and M Mawer, Falmer Press, London

Parry, J (1998) The justification for physical education, in *Physical Education: A reader*, ed K Green and K Hardman, Meyer and Meyer, Aachen, Germany

2 Planning and evaluation

Introduction

Teaching can present a host of challenges, and effective planning can be among the teacher's most valuable tools in meeting those challenges. As every trainee teacher will know, it can become a time-consuming business, but it is usually time well spent. Moreover, planning is one aspect of teachers' work that remains firmly under their direct control.

Objectives

By the end of this chapter you should:

- understand the purposes of planning;
- be aware of the different levels of planning;
- understand the key principles in planning units of work and lesson plans;
- understand the principles of progression;
- understand the purposes and principles of lesson evaluation.

The purposes of planning

Research and simple common sense indicate that effective planning is one of the most significant factors affecting teaching performance. Of course, thorough planning, alone, does not guarantee good teaching and learning, but without it, teaching and learning are severely restricted. Mawer (1995) identifies a host of attributes resulting from appropriate planning by trainee teachers, including:

- greater use of equipment and facilities;
- more directions;
- more careful and precise organization of lessons;
- clearer presentations;
- more specific feedback;
- greater variety and better progression of activities;
- better timing of lessons;
- greater ability to analyse pupils' needs;
- higher levels of activity and time 'on task' among pupils.

Each of these attributes can make a contribution to the success of a lesson and to the quality of pupils' learning.

The process of planning a lesson or a series of lessons allows teachers to articulate their thinking (Williams, 1996a): to think things through carefully and systematically. Thinking through the lesson, its organization and management, its content, its presentation and, most importantly, the things that pupils are supposed to learn from it, can help minimize potential difficulties on the day the lesson is taught. It is always preferable to spot problems *before* a lesson than *during* it!

In planning, the teacher has to make a series of decisions that will determine the character of the lessons. Bailey (2000b) offers a simple way of understanding these decisions. Planning involves:

- decisions about *content*;
- decisions about *organization*;
- decisions about *presentation*.

Decisions about content include:

- What do I want the pupils to learn by the end of this lesson or series of lessons?
- What activities can I select to support this learning?
- How challenging should these activities be for the pupils?
- How much material is it appropriate to include in this lesson or series of lessons?

Decisions about organization include:

- How will the pupils be grouped?
- How shall we use the available space?
- How will the pupils access equipment?
- What are the different roles that the pupils need to take in the lesson?

Decisions about presentation include:

- What is the best way to present the activities to pupils in order to maximize learning?
- How will I present explanations and demonstrations?

- How will the pupils demonstrate their understanding and competence?
- What equipment is most appropriate to support learning?

Thinking teaching through and devising effective strategies at the planning stage can help to reduce the anxiety that naturally arises in inexperienced teachers. Teachers who have planned do not have to worry about every detail of organization, presentation and content when teaching, and so are likely to be much better able to deal with unexpected matters as they arise during the lesson.

The points made so far are reinforced by Clark and Yinger's (1987) summary of the main purposes of planning:

- planning to meet immediate personal needs (eg reduce uncertainty and anxiety, find a sense of direction, confidence and security);
- planning as a means to an end of instruction (learn the material, collect and organize materials, organize time and activity flow);
- direct use of plans during instruction (organize students, get an activity started, aid memory, provide a framework for instruction and evaluation).

Aims and objectives

Planning is an expression of a teacher's intention. It indicates the teacher's decisions about the presentation, organization and content of lessons that promote pupils' learning in the most effective way. Various words are used to represent this intention, such as aims, learning objectives, teaching objectives, intended learning outcomes, purposes and goals. For simplicity, the suggestion of Cohen, Manion and Morrison (1996) will be adopted here. They distinguish between *aims*, which refer to general expressions of intention, and *objectives*, which are characterized by their greater precision and specificity.

Aims form the starting point for curriculum planning. They can vary from very general statements to relatively short-term statements of intention. Examples of long-term aims are the National Curriculum's 'Aims for the school curriculum' (DfEE, 2000): 'Aim 1: The school curriculum should aim to provide opportunities for all pupils to learn and to achieve. Aim 2: The school curriculum should aim to promote pupils' spiritual, moral, social and cultural development and prepare all pupils for the opportunities, responsibilities and experiences of life.'

Long-term aims will usually be reflected in a school or physical education department's policy documentation. As such, they form the basis of the school or department's whole approach to teaching the subject, defining the broad content and character of the provision. The intended learning they represent is understood in terms of pupils' whole time at school. Short-term aims, on the other hand, indicate intended learning and achievement over a specified period of time, such as a term or half-term. They form the starting point for planning schemes or units of work.

Task 2.1

Ask to see the school or physical education department's policy documentation. Which aims does it identify for the physical education curriculum? If there is a list of aims, consider how you would rank them. Which are the most important? Which the least? Which aims can *only* be achieved through physical education?

Discuss the school or department's aims with your mentor.

Objectives are derived from these aims. They are concrete, manageable targets, the reaching of which contributes to the successful achievement of the aims. Objectives are usually expressed in terms of pupils' learning, rather than the teacher's teaching. They can be usefully phrased in the form of some level of understanding or performance that ought to be reached by the end of a specified period of time (for example, by the end of a lesson). The way in which learning objectives contribute to broader aims is illustrated in the box below.

Aim: to develop a simple, controlled gymnastic sequence, using a range of basic actions.

Learning objectives:

- to be able to perform four travelling patterns on the floor;
- to be aware of a variety of linking movements;
- to be able to hold three simple balances with control and articulation;
- to be able to perform three rolling actions, including the forward roll;
- to understand the basic principles of combining basic actions via linking actions.

Cohen, Manion and Morrison (1996) also distinguish between *behavioural objectives* and *non-behavioural objectives*. Behavioural objectives indicate a pupil's explicit achievement, something that can be witnessed, assessed or recorded. For obvious reasons, behavioural objectives are the easiest to monitor, since they express what pupils should be able to do, say or perform by the end of the lesson. Non-behavioural objectives cannot be witnessed directly by the teacher; they are, to some extent, invisible. A great deal of learning in physical education, such as under-standing, attitudes, feelings and values, is not accessible to simple measurement. However, learning of this sort might be reflected in behaviour. For example, whether a child *understands* the importance of breadth of attack in an invasion game, has developed an *appreciation* of a variety of dance styles or has increased *sensitivity* to the feelings of others in adventurous situations might be ascertained by the teacher observing the child *perform* in certain carefully devised activities or by focused questioning. For the purposes of assessment in particular, non-behav-ioural objectives may need to be translated into behavioural objectives (see Figure 2.1).

Units of work

A unit of work represents a series of lessons with a specific group or class based on a unifying theme or topic. The duration of the series can vary from three or four lessons to a term. Whilst an individual lesson plan acts as the most direct source of guidance for teaching, in many ways it is the creation of the unit of work that is the most important. This is because high-quality physical education teaching does not involve presenting a series of discrete, isolated activities. Rather, it is concerned with a systematic introduction and progression through skills and under-standings. So, the teacher needs to plan with an awareness of the contribution that each lesson and activity within it makes and how it relates to the previous and future learning of pupils. Starting planning at the level of units leads the teacher to take the 'bigger picture' of pupil learning. Moreover, once the objectives, progression of activities and appropriate preparations have been determined, planning specific lessons becomes a relatively simple process of adding details of teaching points and organization.

There are many useful formats for presenting units of work (see, for example, Bott, 1997; Bunker, 1994). Figures 2.2 and 2.3 show two examples of units of work framework, the first offering a lesson-by-lesson outline, and the second not sepa-rating the unit into lessons. Of course, schools usually have their own approaches, and trainee and newly qualified teachers will have to work within that approach.

non-behavioural objective

to *understand* the use of extension
and articulation of movement in gymnastics

behavioural objective

to *identify* three good uses of extension
and articulation in a partner's sequence

Figure 2.1   Translation of a non-behavioural objective into a behavioural objective

Theme Age of Pupils		Unit Learning Objectives					
Children with SEN/Medical Conditions		Wider Curricular Opportunities (ICT: Citizenship; Literacy; Numeracy; SMSC)					
Duration of Lesson		Prior Learning and Experience of Theme					
Lesson Structure	Lesson 1	Lesson 2	Lesson 3	Lesson 4	Lesson 5	Lesson 6
Lesson Objectives						
Introduction Development Conclusion						
Resources/ Preparation						
Statutory Requirements				Assessment Criteria			

Figure 2.2 An example lesson-by-lesson framework for a unit of work (adapted from Bailey, 2000b)

There is no perfect template from which it is possible to construct units of work, but there are common features that a teacher needs to include if the unit is to fulfil its function. These features are outlined below.

The first consideration in any planning is pupil learning. It is useful, therefore, to include in a unit of work basic information about the pupils being taught. How old are they? How many pupils are there? How many boys and how many girls? Do any pupils have special educational needs that may be relevant to the content, organization or presentation of lessons? Do any pupils have medical conditions that may be adversely affected by physical activity? The last two points deserve particular attention. No teacher would knowingly place pupils at risk, but they may unwittingly do so if they are unaware of individual pupils' needs. As obvious as this point may be, it is noteworthy how often trainee teachers are presented with a class about which they have been given no information regarding medical conditions or special educational needs.

Theme	Age of Pupils	
	Duration/hours	
Unit Learning Objectives	Attainment Target References	
SEN/Medical Conditions	Prior Learning	

Learning Activities (including differentiation)	Assessment (relate to learning objectives)	Resources/ Preparation

Figure 2.3 A framework for a unit of work

In a similar light, it is important that teachers are aware of pupils' prior learning and experience of the content of the unit, and this is not just to avoid the embarrassment and panic shortly following the words, 'Miss, we did this last term!' Units of work are not delivered in isolation, any more than are lesson plans. It is very rare that a unit introduces a skill or concept that is totally new to pupils, and as pupils progress through their schooling, the probability of previous knowledge and competence increases. As in the case of information of pupils' medical conditions and special educational needs, it is worth while for the trainee or newly qualified teacher to spend some time finding out about pupils' prior experiences of the area about to be taught. Discovering what pupils already know or what they can already do is not always as easy as it sounds. Talking to fellow teachers who have taught the same class and, if possible, consulting their assessment documentation can be very helpful. The simplest and most direct route, of course, is that of talking to the pupils about what is to be taught.

Another important consideration that ought to guide planning relates to any statutory requirements that exist. The National Curriculum for physical education outlines an eight-level attainment target (and an additional level representing exceptional performance), and it is vital that units of work are planned with reference to the attainment target (see box, 'Attainment target for physical education', below). The level descriptions identify clear stages of progression for pupils between 5 and 14 years in relation to four strands:

- acquiring and developing skills;
- selecting and applying skills;
- evaluating and improving skills;
- developing a knowledge and understanding of fitness and health.

Implicit within the level descriptions are stages of progression, which it is necessary to identify and to relate to the learning objectives and the foci for assessment (also see Chapter 8).

Attainment target for physical education

Level 1

Pupils copy, repeat and explore simple skills and actions with basic control and co-ordination. They start to link these skills and actions in ways that suit the activities. They describe and comment on their own and others' actions. They talk about how to exercise safely, and how their bodies feel during an activity.

Level 2

Pupils explore simple skills. They copy, remember, repeat and explore simple actions with control and co-ordination. They vary skills, actions and ideas and link these in ways that suit the activities. They begin to show some understanding of simple tactics and basic compositional ideas. They talk about differences between their own and others' performance and suggest improvements. They understand how to exercise safely, and describe how their bodies feel during different activities.

Level 3

Pupils select and use skills, actions and ideas appropriately, applying them with co-ordination and control. They show that they understand tactics and composition by starting to vary how they respond. They can see how their work is similar to and different from others' work, and use this understanding to improve their own performance. They give reasons why warming up before an activity is important, and why physical activity is good for their health.

Level 4

Pupils link skills, techniques and ideas and apply them accurately and appropriately. Their performance shows precision, control and fluency, and that they understand tactics and composition. They compare and comment on skills, techniques and ideas used in their own and others' work, and use this understanding to improve their performance. They explain and apply basic safety principles in preparing for exercise. They describe what effects exercise has on their bodies, and how it is valuable to their fitness and health.

Level 5

Pupils select and combine their skills, techniques and ideas and apply them accurately and appropriately, consistently showing precision, control and fluency. When performing, they draw on what they know about strategy, tactics and composition. They analyse and comment on skills and techniques and how these are applied in their own and others' work. They modify and refine skills and techniques to improve their performance. They explain how the body reacts during different types of exercise, and warm up and cool down in ways that suit the activity. They explain why regular, safe exercise is good for their fitness and health.

Level 6

Pupils select and combine skills, techniques and ideas. They apply them in ways that suit the activity, with consistent precision, control and fluency. When planning their own and others' work, and carrying out their own work, they draw on what they know about strategy, tactics and composition in response to changing circumstances, and what they know about their own and others' strengths and weaknesses. They analyse and comment on how skills, techniques and ideas have been used in their own and others' work, and on compositional and other aspects of performance, and suggest ways to improve. They explain how to prepare for, and recover from, the activities. They explain how different types of exercise contribute to their fitness and health, and describe how they might get involved in other types of activities and exercise.

Level 7

Pupils select and combine advanced skills, techniques and ideas, adapting them accurately and appropriately to the demands of the activities. They consistently show precision, control, fluency and originality. Drawing on what they know of the principles of advanced tactics and compositional ideas, they apply these in their own and others' work. They modify them in response to changing circumstances and other performers. They analyse and comment on their own and others' work as individuals and team members, showing that they understand how skills, tactics or composition and fitness relate to the quality of the performance. They plan ways to improve their own and others' performance. They explain the principles of practice and training, and apply them effectively. They explain the benefits of regular, planned activity on health and fitness and plan their own appropriate exercise and activity programme.

Level 8

Pupils consistently distinguish and apply advanced skills, techniques and ideas, consistently showing high standards of precision, control, fluency and originality. Drawing on what they know of the principles of advanced tactics or composition, they apply these principles with proficiency and flair in their own and others' work. They adapt it appropriately in response to changing circumstances and other performers. They evaluate their own and others' work, showing that they understand the impact of skills, strategy and tactics or composition, and fitness on the quality and effectiveness of performance. They plan ways in which their own and others' performance could be improved. They create action plans and ways of monitoring improvement. They use their knowledge of health and fitness to plan and evaluate their own and others' exercise and activity programme.

Exceptional performance

Pupils consistently use advanced skills, techniques and ideas with precision and fluency. Drawing on what they know of the principles of advanced strategies and tactics or composition, they consistently apply these principles with originality, proficiency and flair in their own and others' work. They evaluate their own and others' work, showing that they understand how skills, strategy and tactics or composition, and fitness relate to and affect the quality and originality of performance. They reach judgements independently about how their own and others' performance could be improved, prioritizing aspects for further development. They consistently apply appropriate knowledge and understanding of health and fitness in all aspects of their work.

As was discussed in Chapter 1, physical education lessons have enormous potential in contributing to wider educational goals. Some of these goals may be naturally addressed through the context in which physical education is delivered. For example, many activities take place in groups and require a degree of co-operation and communication if they are to take place at all. These are valuable skills for pupils to acquire, and the role that physical education can play should not be underestimated. Other goals may require more deliberate planning, but still demand a place within provision. The sample unit of work (Figure 2.2) includes reference to information and communication technology (ICT), citizenship education, literacy, numeracy, and spiritual, moral, social and cultural development (SMSC). Particularly at the primary phase, where there is a less strict separation between subjects and where a single individual usually teaches the whole curriculum, this might be extended to include other curriculum areas, like geography and music. Two important cross-curricular areas, ICT and citizenship education, are addressed in detail in Chapters 9 and 10 respectively. Other examples of cross-curricular approaches are discussed in Chapter 1.

In the context of the earlier discussion of aims and objectives, National Curriculum requirements determine the aims of the unit of work. The teacher then has to decide which learning objectives can act as smaller, more focused targets for pupils' learning, towards the achievement of the aims. Unlike aims, which are necessarily long-term, objectives have to be achievable within the duration of the unit or the lesson. Indeed, it is a useful strategy to phrase learning objectives in that way: 'By the end of this unit (or lesson), pupils should understand/demonstrate/perform...'

Once learning objectives have been identified, the next step is to select appropriate activities or tasks. The identification of learning objectives will normally precede the selection of specific material or content. Starting with objectives forces the teacher to think about different ways of achieving those objectives, and this is likely to result in greater variety in lesson content. In practice, some teachers begin their course planning with initial decisions about content to be taught and teaching context, and only later turn to aims and objectives (Taylor, 1970), but this is not likely to be the most effective approach for trainee and newly qualified teachers.

A good unit of work indicates continuity and progression. In other words, it demonstrates how individual lessons and their constituent parts are logically related to one another, and how the achievement of earlier objectives and activities is developed into later ones. A great deal of learning in physical education is progressive in this way. For example, before pupils can maintain a complex balance with a narrow base, they will usually need to master holding simpler balances with wider bases. Units of work, therefore, need to reflect a progression of activities, and the development from lesson to lesson should present manageable steps for the pupils. (See the next section for further guidance on progression.)

A unit of work should give some indication of the organizational factors and teaching approaches involved in its delivery. Lesson plans should contain the greatest detail of these aspects of planning. However, it is worth while to offer some coverage at the level of the unit, not least because it offers the teacher a valuable opportunity to reflect upon the variety of learning contexts pupils will encounter.

Finally, it is essential to give some attention to the way in which learning will be assessed. Objectives specify targets for learning that the teacher intends pupils to achieve by the end of the unit, and so it is important that criteria for assessment are identified at the planning stage. This process can be summarized as in Figure 2.4.

Figure 2.4 The aims to assessment process

The box below offers a summary of the information that usually needs to be included in a unit of work, whatever the framework adopted.

Information to include in a unit of work:

1. details about the class:
   - year/age;
   - number of pupils in group (boys/girls);
   - special educational needs;
   - medical conditions;
   - ability (if appropriate);
2. group's previous experience of the unit theme;
3. number and length of the lessons in the unit;
4. statutory requirements (eg eight-stage attainment target);
5. opportunities to contribute to wider educational goals, including to information and communication technology, citizenship education, literacy, numeracy, and spiritual, moral, social and cultural development;
6. learning objectives to be achieved by the end of the unit;
7. brief outline of the content of the lesson in the unit;
8. indication of the progression of objectives and activities throughout the unit;
9. organizational factors and teaching approaches to be used (eg individual, paired or group activities, direct or indirect teaching styles);
10. resources required;
11. criteria for assessment – how pupils' learning and achievement will be assessed against the learning objectives.

Progression

As stated earlier, it is important to plan units of work with reference to well-articulated learning objectives. The individual lesson plans that develop from the unit can be seen as stepping stones towards the achievement of these objectives, and so it is important that lessons and their activities progress in a logical manner. Siedentop (1991: 289) has suggested that the planning of the unit is developed by 'working backwards from the final performance description to where the unit begins'. In other words, teachers should begin by asking themselves, 'Where do I wish the pupils to reach by the end of the unit?' They then ask, 'What are the best ways to get them there?'

Planning individual tasks and even lessons can be a relatively simple process. However, planning a series of tasks or lessons in a progressive sequence can be challenging. Indeed, the National Curriculum Council (NCC, 1992) describes this aspect of planning as one of the biggest problems for teachers. There have been various solutions to this problem (see, for example, Mawer, 1995 and Rink, 1993). The model that will be considered here is that of Williams (1996a), who has suggested that progression can take at least three forms: the difficulty of the tasks achieved; the quality of the response; and the context in which it is reproduced.

Progression through difficulty can be seen when pupils are required to perform increasingly challenging tasks, such as:

- moving from single to combined movements (eg balance – balance to roll – balance to roll to balance);
- moving from relatively simple to relatively advanced skills (eg basic throwing action – specialized throwing action – javelin);
- performing a task with reduced time (eg time limit for possession of ball in a passing game);
- performing a task with reduced space (eg restricting playing area);
- performing with a reduced choice of options (eg devising gymnastics sequence using only certain body shapes);
- developing from concrete to more abstract or strategic approaches (eg discussing feelings and ideas for a dance);
- responding in a greater variety of ways to a challenge (eg 'How many different ways can you think of for moving across the mat?').

Progression in quality can be seen when pupils demonstrate increasingly more sophisticated or successful performance. Examples of progression in quality include:

- better poise, control and form in movement in gymnastics or dance performance;
- improved accuracy in target games;
- more refined movements in the execution of swimming strokes;
- faster times or greater distances achieved in athletics activities;
- increased fluency in skill performance.

Progression in context can be seen when pupils are able to carry out skills in increasingly complex situations. Examples include:

- working individually, then with a partner, then in a small group and then in a larger group;
- working individually and then co-operatively;
- taking greater responsibility in the planning, performance and evaluation of activities;
- applying skills in a variety of contexts;
- understanding a wider variety of roles within games playing.

Lesson plans

'Effective teachers plan! No matter what method they use to teach or how independent they become of actual physical lesson plans, they all carefully consider objectives and activities, progressions, equipment and space needs, safety and managerial issues and evaluation' (Siedentop, 1991: 185).

Once teachers have planned their units of work and determined their learning objectives, they are ready to plan lessons. It is worth spending time planning units in some detail, as this makes lesson planning much easier and less stressful. As Siedentop's statement suggests, even experienced teachers recognize the value of well-thought-out plans. For trainee and inexperienced teachers, they can make the difference between success and failure.

A guiding principle is that the less experienced the teacher, the more detailed the plans should be. More experienced colleagues have a great deal of knowledge and skill related to class organization and presentation, and many of their practices have become automatic and need not be written down. This is not the case for trainee and newly qualified teachers, who more often rely upon the support of detailed plans. A useful strategy for trainee teachers early in their school experience is to show their plans to a colleague. Could they teach from the plans, with only the information provided on them for guidance? If they could not, then there is probably a need for more detail.

The need for detailed plans should not be understood as a call for inflexibility. The lesson plan is the most up-to-date form of planning that teachers have at their disposal. Whilst it is possible to plan units of work some time in advance of teaching, lesson plans should reflect teachers' most recent knowledge of the pupils. So, a trainee teacher who completes all lesson planning before actually meeting the pupils is courting disaster. Detailed plans written in advance of teaching cannot be responsive to emerging pupil needs and events. What happens if the pupils need to spend more time than anticipated to complete the first stage of the unit? What if a widespread misconception of a crucial point becomes apparent? What if pupils have already done the planned activities before to a satisfactory standard? It is better to write fairly flexible plans, which are made more detailed nearer the time of teaching.

There are numerous different lesson plan formats (an example is provided in Figure 2.5). Their design can vary with the activity area being taught, the age of the pupils, school/university template, type of lesson and teacher preference. Nevertheless, there are certain features of lesson planning that ought to be addressed in any plan, and these are discussed in this section.

Lesson Plan			
Theme:		Date/Time:	
Learning Objectives:		Class/No of Pupils:	

References to Statutory Requirements:

Resources and Lesson Preparation:

Phase/Timing	Pupils' Activities	Teaching and Safety Points	Assessment
Introduction (Warm-up)			
Development			
Conclusion (Cool-down)			

Figure 2.5   An example lesson plan template

Lesson structure

There is an old adage relating to the way teachers ought to sequence their teaching: *'Tell them what you are going to tell them... Tell them... Tell them what you told them!'* In other words, start a lesson by introducing the pupils to the things they are about to do and learn. Then present the content of the lesson. Finally, recap the important features that have been done and learnt during the lesson. As simplistic as it sounds, this provides a very useful model for lesson design, and reflects the three main phases within physical education lessons:

- introduction;
- development;
- conclusion.

The total length of the lesson can vary considerably, from 20 minutes to over an hour. Younger children can experience difficulties attending to overlong lessons. For example, Hopper, Grey and Maude (2000) suggest that five-year-olds may be able to sustain only 20 minutes of activity, and that 10 minutes of outside games may be more appropriate than half an hour inside. Older children should be able to deal with longer lessons. Indeed, greater time is often necessary if they are to practise and develop their skills.

The *introduction* is a vital, yet frequently underused, part of the lesson. Teachers can be so eager to get the children active that they fail to introduce the lesson to pupils. Rink (1993) uses the term 'set induction' to refer to the process of orientating the learners to work they will be doing during the lesson, and why it is important. There is a great deal of evidence showing that learning is significantly enhanced when learners understand the purpose of the activities they are performing (Barnsford, Brown and Cocking, 1999). One way of achieving this is by relating the lesson to previous work: 'Do you remember last week when we practised different ways of rolling? Well, today we are going to look at different starting and finishing positions for our rolls, and how we can link them with other actions to make sequences.'

Another function of the introductory phase is to prepare the class physically for movement. The need to warm-up is a distinctive feature of physical education practical lessons. The selection of activities for the warm-up will depend upon many factors, such as the age of the children and the tasks they are about to perform. One approach is to break the warm-up into two parts: the first part includes a range of aerobic activities to raise the heart and breathing rates steadily and warm the muscles and tendons; the second part includes some physical conditioning exercises, such as stretching and/or strengthening activities.

Warming-up activities should reflect the sorts of activities that will occur during the main phase of the lesson. This ensures that the relevant muscle groups are prepared for action. Generic activities, such as running around the outside of the area, are of limited value in this respect. It is preferable to give pupils a taste of the lesson to come, and to allow them to experience the equipment they will use.

Task 2.2

Devising appropriate warm-ups is an art in itself. Over time, you will build up your own collection of activities, and this collection can be started now. With reference to some of the books in the 'References' and 'Further reading' sections of this book, and through discussion with your colleagues, start to compile a list of warm-up activities. Be specific regarding their application. In preparation for which sort of lesson might they be used? For what age pupils are they appropriate?

Once the introduction has finished, pupils progress to the *development* phase of the lesson. It is at this stage, which takes up the greatest proportion of the lesson, that they most explicitly work towards the lesson objectives. Rather than conceiving of the development phase as one block of time, it can be useful to divide it into distinct parts, and design a progression through them so that they make coherent and intellectual sense to the pupils and support learning (Kyriacou, 1991). The conventional way of doing this in the areas of games, gymnastics and dance is shown in Figure 2.6.

Not all lessons will develop in this way. Some gymnastics lessons may include only floorwork or apparatus work; some dance lessons may consist almost entirely of the practice and presentation of a previously devised dance.

There may be good reason to challenge the conventional wisdom of games planning. Most writers on the subject have argued that it is important that the skill learning part of a lesson should precede the performance of that skill in a game. Gallahue (1993: 198) writes that 'only after the skill has been mastered should it be incorporated into game-like activities'. Countering this, Bailey (2000b) has

Games	Gymnastics	Dance
development:	development:	development:
1) skill learning	1) floorwork	1) movement ideas
↓↓↓↓	↓↓↓↓	↓↓↓↓
2) small-sided games	2) apparatus	2) dance

Figure 2.6   Development in games, gymnastics and dance

suggested that playing the game itself creates the context for any associated skill learning. In other words, pupils will have little understanding of when and why to use skills, unless they understand how to apply them within the game. By starting the development phase of the lesson with a simple game activity, the teacher is able to illustrate the sort of situation in which the skill will be used. Alternatively, specific skills can be offered as solutions to problems encountered by the players. This helps create meaningful learning experiences for pupils, and research suggests that meaningful experiences are most effective for learning and recall (Barnsford, Brown and Cocking, 1999):

> (*During a tennis lesson*)
> *Teacher*: There have been some really good strokes played, and some exciting rallies! But one thing I've noticed is that a lot of you seem to be finding it difficult to control the power of your drop shots at the net. Let's just take a break from the game for a few minutes to practise this exercise that should improve your drop shots.

This sort of approach has been found to be a particularly useful strategy with younger children, pupils with learning difficulties and those with behavioural difficulties. By starting with the 'point' of the lesson (the game), and only later moving on to isolated skills, it can be easier for pupils to understand the *application* of the skill, rather than simply the mechanics of the action.

Following this model, the development phase of learning might be structured as in Figure 2.7.

The final phase of the lesson is the *conclusion*. There are sound physiological as well as educational reasons for making sure that every lesson has an adequate conclusion. Many physical education lessons involve vigorous activities, and it is important that pupils are given the chance to cool down their bodies and lower their heart and breathing rates before leaving the lesson. Gentle, rhythmic exercises, such

development:

game

↓ ↓ ↓ ↓

skill learning

↓ ↓ ↓ ↓

game

Figure 2.7 Development starting with the game

as stretches, can also calm pupils, which may be particularly important with young children, as they can become very excited during lessons.

The conclusion is an opportunity to recap on the lesson, for pupils to reflect upon the activities and for the teacher to assess understanding and to orient for the next lesson:

- 'Who can tell me something that you have learnt in this lesson?'
- 'In pairs, tell each other two points to remember when playing a backhand stroke.'
- 'Today, we composed sequences with a few actions. Next week, we are going to explore ways of developing longer and more complex sequences.'

Other aspects of the lesson plan

The *learning objectives* for the lesson are determined by those for the broader unit of work. Since an individual lesson is really part of a progressive series, learning objectives should develop skills and understanding from earlier learning. Objectives state the knowledge, understanding, skills and attitudes that the teacher intends pupils to acquire or develop during the lesson, and so should be phrased accordingly: 'By the end of the lesson, pupils should be able to list three short-term effects of exercise on the body.'

Preparation for physical education lessons is generally quite considerable in comparison to other subjects. Adequate preparation of equipment can make a significant contribution to pupils' levels of activity and consequently learning (Hellison and Templin, 1991). Conversely, poor preparation can lead to wasted time, misbehaviour and accidents.

The teacher needs to think carefully about matching the equipment to the age and ability of the pupils. Equipment that is of inappropriate size, weight or shape can hinder learning. It is also important that enough equipment is available for the activities planned. A teacher suddenly disappearing into the store for a few extra balls or mats is usually the signal for bad behaviour, or at least pupils standing around doing nothing.

Placement of equipment is another consideration that ought be thought through at the lesson planning stage. Gymnastics apparatus lessons clearly need layouts devised in advance of the lesson. But there is also a need in other situations, especially when pupils need to access equipment. Kit that is piled in a corner or, even worse, in a cupboard becomes a hazard when 30 pupils are told to 'get a ball each' and they descend upon it simultaneously. A much better approach is for the teacher to distribute equipment around the outside of the area (space permitting). A sketch of equipment layout can be drawn on the reverse of the lesson plan.

Different types of lessons will have different *timings* for the phases of the lesson. Generally speaking, the introductory and concluding phases should be quite brief, leaving the majority of lesson time to the development phase.

Inexperienced teachers will find it very helpful to supplement their description of activities in the lesson with *teaching and safety points*. These highlight important aspects of delivery or organization that make sure the lesson is carried out in as safe and successful a way as possible. Key points of skills and techniques can be included, and can be reminders of specific concepts and vocabulary that ought to be emphasized.

Good physical education lessons are characterized by learning, and not just activity. In order to determine whether the lesson has been effective in facilitating pupils' learning, *assessment data* need to be gathered on performance and progress. Observations and questioning during the lesson can provide useful information. However, pupils can be very skilled at concealing their lack of understanding (Pye, 1988), so a more structured approach is necessary. Perhaps the simplest way is to specify when the pupils' achievement of the lesson's learning objectives will be assessed. (Assessment will be discussed in Chapter 8.)

Improving lesson planning

Three other features of effective lesson planning need to be considered: transitions, scripting of input and dealing with non-performers.

It is during the periods of *transition* between one activity and the next that many behavioural and safety problems arise (Bailey, 2000b). It is easy for adults to under-estimate the difficulty children can have in changing groups or in getting new equipment. Consider the following example from a Year 7 tennis lesson:

- Activity 1 – warm-up exercise: one ball and one racket per pupil; pupils bounce the ball at various heights, and on alternate faces of the racket.
- Activity 2 – skill learning: in pairs, pupils practise a co-operative rally over the net.

The transition from one activity to the next can present a number of organizational issues for the teacher:

- How do the pupils get into pairs?
- Who decides the pairings?
- What do they do with the extra ball?
- How do they find a place at the net?
- What happens if there is not enough space at the net for all pairs?

Each issue could lead to delay or misbehaviour in the lesson. It is far better that they are thought through at the planning stage than during the actual lesson.

Task 2.3

How would you answer these questions if you were delivering the activities suggested above?

A similar planning 'safety net' is the idea of *scripting of input*. Everyone has been in a situation where they suddenly forgot what they were about to say. In most cases, this can be a little embarrassing. Faced with a class full of lively, excited and perhaps mischievous pupils, the consequences can be more severe. Writing out every word to be spoken during the lesson is impractical (probably impossible). However, there may be sections of the lesson where it may be helpful to have access to written notes, especially if the material is complex (such as some of the scientific content of GCSE and A level syllabi) or when great accuracy is essential (such as when outlining games rules).

A final point relates to those pupils who are unable to participate in activities, perhaps owing to injury and illness. This should be quite a rare occurrence: generally speaking, if pupils are well enough to be at school, they are well enough to join in physical education lessons. However, there are exceptions to this rule, such as broken bones, and the teacher needs to be able to offer meaningful work for non-participants. As was discussed in Chapter 1, the National Curriculum for physical education envisages pupils engaging in a continuous process of planning, performing and evaluating. One way of planning for these *non-performers* is by focusing upon the other parts of the cycle: planning and evaluating. In this way, all pupils can engage with the intended learning, albeit in different ways. There are countless learning opportunities for non-performers. A few are listed below:

- Help a partner plan a gymnastics sequence or dance routine.
- Devise tactics.
- Act as a coach with a group, using teaching points given by the teacher.
- Devise apparatus layout for a future lesson.
- Describe, using appropriate technical language, an observed activity.
- Provide feedback on peers' performance.
- Assess performance, using teaching points given by the teacher.
- Use a camcorder to record and offer feedback for participants.

The box below offers a summary of the information that usually needs to be included in a lesson plan.

Information to include in a lesson plan:

- statement of learning objectives;
- indication of topic of lesson;
- indication of relevant statutory requirements;
- prior learning or experience of pupils;
- resources and lesson preparation;
- date/time available;
- planned timing of phases and activities;
- activities to be undertaken by pupils;
- organizational factors (eg grouping, access to resources, transitions);
- specific teaching points to be raised during lesson;
- indication of how differentiation will be addressed;
- anticipated problems and safety issues;
- indication of evidence that can contribute to assessment of learning.

Evaluation of lessons

'The best teachers combine their talent, enthusiasm, hard work, personality and perseverance with a willingness to think about their work and make improvements on the basis of advice from others and intelligent reflection' (Hayes, 1999: 105).

Without critical reflection upon their teaching, it is unlikely that anyone would improve their performance. Evaluations provide an opportunity to scrutinize practice honestly and constructively, acknowledging strengths and weaknesses and searching for better ways to operate in the future. Evaluations from mentors and tutors provide expert feedback on a range of teaching matters, but self-evaluation is of particular benefit, as it is self-initiated, frequent and often blunt.

Good evaluations have a number of qualities, including:

- They are focused.
- They should be analytical, rather than just descriptive.
- They are reasonable: they don't expect perfection.
- They record both success and failure.
- They should be formative: they should significantly influence future planning and teaching.

There are many different evaluation formats (see, for example, Moyles, 1988; Hayes, 2000; Cohen, Manion and Morrison, 1996). One approach, derived from the planning model presented in this book, evaluates in terms of three broad areas:

- content;
- organization;
- presentation.

Content

- Did all/most/some/none of the pupils achieve the learning objectives?
- Was my subject knowledge adequate for the lesson and the class?
- Were my feedback and guidance accurate and concise?
- Was my use of questioning effective?
- Did the selected activities facilitate achievement of the objectives?
- Was the pace of the lesson appropriate?
- Did I modify activities for different abilities?
- Was the introduction crisp and engaging?
- Were all pupils properly warmed up?
- Were the series of development activities coherent?
- Were all children physically active for most of the lesson?
- Did the lesson conclude purposefully and positively?
- Did the lesson build on previous learning and experience?
- Did I allow sufficient time for tasks?
- Did the assessment data prove relevant and manageable?

Organization

- Were groupings of pupils effective?
- Did I use the PE area effectively?
- Could pupils understand the organization strategies?
- Did pupils behave appropriately?
- Were my discipline strategies effective?
- Were transitions smooth and controlled?
- Was I positioned so that I could observe all of the pupils?
- Did any tasks take longer to organize than expected?
- Was safety monitored at all times?
- Were spatial boundaries identified and observed?
- Could pupils move around the space when necessary?

Presentation

- Was I appropriately dressed?
- Were resources readily available and suitable to the age and level of the pupils?
- Were explanations of tasks clear and unambiguous?
- Were all children listening and able to hear?
- Were the teaching strategies and styles appropriate for the objectives and activities?
- Did I use a variety of teaching styles?
- Were demonstrations used effectively?
- Were other adults utilized effectively?
- Did I show enthusiasm?
- Was praise used appropriately?
- Did I develop a rapport with the class?
- Did I use my voice, posture and gestures effectively?

Task 2.4

1. Referring to the guidance provided above, evaluate a recent lesson, using the following headings for your comments:
   - content;
   - organization;
   - presentation.
2. Using the same headings, evaluate another lesson. This time, ask your mentor or a colleague to carry out an evaluation of the same lesson. Discuss similarities and differences in your evaluations. Who was most critical? Were any issues missed in your evaluations?

Of course, these are only some of the questions a teacher might ask when evaluating a lesson. Later chapters will discuss different aspects of teaching physical education in detail, and as you work through them you will think of other questions. Perfection is an unattainable goal, but the good teacher is able to continue to improve performance through a combination of honest evaluation and a positive attitude.

Summary

This chapter has suggested a range of approaches to planning in physical education lessons. It has suggested that effective planning is one of the most important skills that teachers of physical education can acquire. Main points *to* remember include the following:

- Planning can be for both the short and long term, and involves decisions about content, organization and presentation of lessons.
- Teachers should plan for activities that are progressively more challenging for pupils.
- Evaluations, both by others and by oneself, can be a valuable tool for the improvement of teaching.

Further reading

Bailey, R P (2000) Planning and preparation for effective teaching, in *Teaching Physical Education 5–11*, ed R P Bailey and T M Macfadyen, Continuum, London

Kyriacou, C (1991) *Essential Teaching Skills*, Chapter 2, Simon and Schuster, Hemel Hempstead

Mawer, M (1995) *The Effective Teaching of Physical Education*, Chapter 5, Longman, London

3 Promoting a positive climate for learning

Introduction

'Physical Education classes should be characterized by an environment that is conducive to learning. [PE areas] should be places where all students can have positive experiences. Teachers and students should enjoy being there' (Rink, 1993: 127).

This chapter examines ways in which teachers can promote and maintain lesson climates that support learning in physical education. As Rink's quotation implies, positive and supportive climates for learning can significantly affect the ways in which both pupils and teachers approach lessons. As such, they are important factors in promoting learning and appropriate behaviour.

Objectives

By the end of this chapter you should:

- understand the importance and character of positive learning climates in physical education lessons;
- understand the importance of appropriate interpersonal relationships between teachers and pupils;
- understand the importance of high expectations for pupils' achievement;
- be familiar with strategies for expressing authority as a teacher;
- know ways of helping pupils to focus upon the task at hand;
- know ways of maintaining on-task behaviour.

Positive climates

The climate of a lesson is its general atmosphere or tone. A climate that is positive and supportive can have a great influence on the motivation of pupils and their attitude to learning. Kyriacou (1991: 60) characterizes a successful classroom climate as being 'purposeful, task-orientated, relaxed, warm, supportive and [with a] sense of order'.

Task 3.1

Consider the elements of Kyriacou's description of a successful classroom climate:

- purposeful;
- task-orientated;
- relaxed;
- warm;
- supportive;
- sense of order.

1. How would an observer recognize these qualities in the context of a physical education lesson? Against each of the elements, list the sort of behaviours of the teacher and pupils that would be seen.
2. Ask your mentor or a colleague to observe one of your lessons, using these elements as criteria for their evaluation. How well did you generate an environment that was task-orientated, relaxed and so on?

Some teachers are very good at creating a strong sense of purpose in their lessons. Some promote a supportive and caring environment. Good teachers do both. Research certainly suggests that this is the view of pupils. For example, Saunders (1979) reviewed the findings of studies of pupils' descriptions of 'good' teachers, and constructed the following picture. Good teachers:

- are purposeful and in control of themselves;
- know what they want to teach and check that the pupils are learning;
- take positive action when they discover pupils are not making adequate progress;
- are sensitive to the reactions of the pupils and respond by changing role smoothly and appropriately;
- try to understand the point of view of the learner;

- show respect for others;
- are concerned for all the pupils.

In other words, according to pupils, good teachers represent a combination of purposefulness and sensitivity.

Teachers need to give the impression that they are in control of their lessons, that time must not be wasted and that nothing ought to interfere with the important business of learning. A businesslike style of presentation can contribute to the general sense of purpose in the lesson, and this is most likely to occur when the teacher is in control of behaviour from the moment the pupils enter the physical education area, knows the subject and has thoroughly planned the lesson (see Chapter 2), is appropriately dressed and conveys confidence, enthusiasm and energy.

According to the humorous stereotype, physical education teachers might be the last people to be described as sensitive and caring. However, it is possible to argue that sensitivity on the part of the teacher is more important in physical education lessons than in any other subject, since it presents pupils with unique physical and emotional challenges, some involving an element of adventure and apparent risk. Moreover, there is an unprecedented emphasis upon public displays of ability. Overall, the subject demands that the teacher exhibits warmth, reassurance, kindness and tact; what Pye (1988: 2) calls 'solicitous tenderness'.

Interpersonal relationships

A factor that is likely to have a considerable effect upon the climate of the lesson is the type of relationship that has been established between the teacher and the pupils. Positive and appropriate relationships are characterized by mutual respect. These sorts of relationships do not happen by accident: teachers need to plan and monitor their development. Some trainee teachers find it difficult to gauge an appropriate style of communication, and their behaviour sometimes falls into over-friendliness. This can break down the necessary distinction between teacher and learner, which can result in discipline problems that endanger any positive climate that may have developed.

Siedentop (1991: 132) suggested a number of strategies that teachers can use to develop appropriate relationships with their pupils:

- Know your pupils.
- Appreciate your pupils.
- Acknowledge their efforts.
- Be a careful listener.

- Include pupils in decisions.
- Make some concessions when appropriate.
- Always show respect for pupils.
- Show honesty and integrity.
- Develop a sense of community, of belonging to the class.

Learning pupils' names can make a particularly valuable contribution to lesson climate. It indicates to pupils that the teacher sees them as individuals, rather than merely as a group, and this, in turn, suggests a degree of knowledge and understanding of their unique needs. This is much easier for primary school teachers than for their secondary colleagues, who will teach numerous different groups during a week. Nevertheless, teachers in both phases need to spend time learning pupils' names. There are a number of approaches to help teachers learn and recall names (see, for example, Capel, Leask and Turner, 1995), and it is worth experimenting to find out one that works.

Task 3.2

Once you have worked with a class for a while, try the following exercise. Using the class register to make sure no one is omitted, try to identify a strength, talent or personal interest for every pupil in the class. Are there any groups of pupils who are very easy to get to know? Are there any pupils about whom you know very little? Return to it from time to time, and notice how your answers change or develop.

This task illustrates a key insight into effective teacher–pupil relationships, namely that they involve treating and valuing pupils as individuals with distinctive qualities and characteristics. This is well put by Dawney (1977):

For a child to develop and function as a person, he needs to be treated as someone who is important in his own right and not just as a member of a category. He needs help in developing the kind of self-concept that allows him to regard himself as of value. To treat children as persons in their own right involves regarding them as responsible for their own actions and therefore having some control over what they do.

A sense of humour can be an invaluable skill for the teacher. Of course, not all humour is appropriate in the context of teacher–pupil relationships, and certain jokes can be seen as upsetting or even offensive by some pupils. Nevertheless, when used sensibly, humour can be a useful strategy for defusing tense situations, or simply helping to maintain a pleasant, positive learning environment. It is also a way of portraying an image of relaxation and confidence, both of which suggest a teacher in control of the lesson.

Teacher–pupil relationships can be established in numerous ways, and teachers who have positive relationships with their pupils often foster and cement them in different social contexts (Cohen, Manion and Morrison, 1996). Physical education teachers are particularly well placed to do this, and their contact with pupils frequently extends beyond lessons. Some of the ways in which good teacher–pupil relationships can develop include:

- taking time to talk to pupils whilst supervising break periods;
- organizing and supporting extra-curricular sports clubs;
- travelling with teams to inter-school competitions;
- taking an interest in the sporting and recreational interests of the pupils;
- sharing jokes and anecdotes;
- talking to pupils as they enter the lesson about what they did at the weekend or the outcome of an event.

Expressing authority

Capel, Kelly and Whitehead (1997: 100) have argued that physical education teachers need to be 'confident, authoritative and clearly in control of the situation'. Aside from the general principle that all teachers should act as figures of authority, physical education presents further demands, since the subject usually takes place in a large space, within which pupils can be widely distributed, and in an environment that might contain safety hazards. So, it is vital that teachers establish and communicate their authority at all stages of teaching physical education, although the nature of that authority may vary with the age of the pupils.

Communication is made up of much more than simply the words used. Words and phrases can convey different meanings for the listener, depending upon a host of other factors, such as tone of voice and body language. Consider the word 'Hello'. By changing the way it is spoken, it can be an acknowledgement, exclamation of surprise, flirtation, greeting or threat. Everybody uses different tones of voice and gestures to communicate meaning, and often without any thought at all. This is supported by some research (reported in O'Connor and Seymour, 1993) suggesting that, in a presentation before a group, words account for only a small proportion of the impact of the communication. Much more influential are body language and tone of voice (see Figure 3.1).

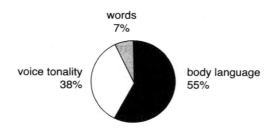

Figure 3.1   Impact of presentation

While we are all quite comfortable with subtleties of communication in everyday life, teaching presents new communication challenges to most trainees and those new to the profession. So, it is worth spending a little time reflecting upon the use of voice and body language to convey meaning to pupils. Expressing authority is an important case in point.

The expression of authority is a skill that some trainee and newly qualified teachers find problematic. Wragg and Wood (1984a: 9) suggest that this is because they themselves are not clear about the form and nature of the relationship and all that it entails. Effective teachers express and reinforce a consistent message about their authority. Ineffective teachers behave inconsistently, and present contradictory messages. This confuses pupils, and prompts some to test how much authority the teacher is willing to concede.

Simply being a teacher empowers an individual with certain institutional authority and legal powers. In the past, this was supported by a great deal of respect shown towards teachers by pupils and the wider community. As Tattum (1982) pointed out, however, this has now changed: 'Respect for the teacher *qua* teacher can no longer be assumed as a social fact. No longer is the office held in awe and teachers who draw heavily upon unquestioned authority as an endowed right leave themselves open to mimicry and ridicule.' A great deal of the personal authority of teachers rests upon the effectiveness of their teaching, together with the concern they show for pupils and their welfare (Robertson, 1989). However, teaching alone will not always result in respect from pupils. Other factors play a role, too, such as use of language, eye contact, tone of voice, use of space and personal appearance. These factors will be examined below.

Voice

Clarity is an essential quality of teachers' speech. If pupils can't hear or understand teachers, they will not be in a position to do what is required of them. Lack of clarity in speech is often a matter of habit, and, as such, it is something of which speakers are unaware. This is because speakers' perceptions of how they sound can be very different from the way they sound to others. The next task asks you to tape-record yourself speaking or teaching. Most people (almost everyone, in fact) are shocked when they hear themselves for the first time, since their voices sound nothing like they imagined. They might find that their voice sounds slower, squeakier or more mumbled than they thought. They might also discover the repeated use of particular words or phrases, like 'OK', 'all right', 'um', 'er' and so on.

In the speakers' defence it ought to be recognized that even a tape recorder fails to offer an exact reproduction of a voice, since it is more sensitive to certain frequencies of sound than others. The voices of women, in particular, seem to come out higher on a tape recording than they actually are (Berry, 1994). Also, as was discussed above, people don't just communicate with their voices. Eye contact, gestures and other forms of non-verbal communication all contribute to the message put across to others.

Bearing these cautions in mind, taping one's voice is still an extremely useful exercise. Other useful exercises are suggested in various voice-training guides, such as *Your Voice and How To Use It* by Cecily Berry (1994).

Task 3.3

Tape-record yourself speaking; brace yourself and play back the recording. It is best to record yourself speaking in a number of different contexts (at home, at school, in the gym, in the classroom) to hear how your voice varies.

If you identify specific points for development, focus on just one at a time. Either re-record yourself after you have practised for a while, or ask your mentor or another colleague to listen and give feedback.

It is important to keep a sense of proportion with this exercise. Most people are alarmed when they hear their voice for the first time, and this is perfectly natural. It should not lead to excessive self-consciousness or lack of confidence.

Some teachers compare their role to that of an actor. For example, Ross (1978) makes the following statement, in relation to lecturing: 'One writes "performance" because this is what a good lecture often is. The language of the theatre does not come amiss here; the tyro is directed not to turn his back on the audience, to articulate clearly, to project, to maintain eye contact, to practise timing, to use gestures appropriately, to relate to his audience, etc, etc.'

Other teachers object to this type of comparison, claiming that it underplays the importance of genuine personal relationships. They point out that an 'act' can only be maintained for a limited period, and that the teacher's true personality will come through in the end. These are reasonable points, but they do not negate the central issue: effective teaching requires the development of special qualities, including speaking and listening skills, the ability to establish and maintain control, and the effective selection and presentation of content. None of these is particularly easy for most people, and all demand thought and effort.

The effective use of voice is an essential skill for all teachers. The voice coach, Sonia Woolley (quoted in the *Times Educational Supplement*, December 2000: 12), makes the point well: 'The greatest tool teachers have is the way they communicate and the thing that does that is the voice.' Physical education teachers have a particularly great need to develop effective speaking skills. They use their voices in a greater variety of environments than other teachers, from the gymnasium, to the field, to the classroom, to the swimming pool. Each of these different settings requires the teacher to vary volume, pitch, tone, speed and emphasis when talking to pupils.

Moments of silence can also be valuable. They break the pattern of talk, and can make the listener focus more intently on what is coming next. Combined with emphasis, pauses can help pupils focus upon key points. As an example, consider the following extract from a teacher's intervention during a Key Stage 3 rugby lesson:

> There is some very good running with the ball, and I am *very* [emphasis] pleased to see so many of you remembering to use the width of the playing area. *But* [emphasis], many of you are still forgetting to do a *really* [emphasis] important thing. [Pause.] It is vital that you remember to [pause] look [pause]. *Look* [emphasis] before you pass. Too often, people are just throwing the ball into thin air, or to the other side! As you play, I want to see everybody remembering to [pause] look [pause]. *Look* [emphasis] before you pass.

Body language

As with the voice, the messages communicated by the body are often things of which many people are unaware. However, as was shown above, body language plays a great role in effective communication. Sotto (1994: 150) notes, 'The way teachers communicate in a lesson surely conveys much more than facts or ideas. It conveys the kind of people they are and how they feel about other people. It also conveys the kind of attitude toward learning and teaching they have and the kind of values they hold.' There is a great deal of non-verbal communication taking place during every physical education lesson, on the part of both teachers and pupils.

Non-verbal communication can reveal a great deal about the inner state of an individual. Consider two teachers at the start of the year. The first stands in a prominent position before the class, with a moderately relaxed posture and facial expression. This teacher looks around the group as they enter the gym and sit down, making momentary eye contact with some pupils and smiling in a welcoming manner. The second stands to the side of the group, with hands folded across the chest, head slightly bowed. This teacher does not make eye contact with the pupils, and maintains a tense facial expression. What messages might the pupils pick up about the confidence and authority of these two teachers?

Robertson (1989) discusses ways in which status difference is conveyed through different forms of posture and eye contact. There is an association between an erect posture and signs of respect and attention. So, experienced teachers often appear quite relaxed in front of a class, whilst expecting the pupils to greet them in an attentive way by sitting upright and looking directly at them.

Task 3.4

An interesting exercise is to watch a film or television programme with the volume turned off. What clues are offered to indicate the differences in status between the characters on the screen? Look particularly at the ways the characters use eye contact, gestures, the direction they face and personal space.

The use of eye contact plays a very significant role in effective class management and control. A number of studies have shown it to be a valuable tool for teachers. For example, in their study of experienced teachers' early encounters with a new class, Wragg and Wood (1984a) found that many emphasized using their eyes to emphasize that they were 'in charge'. One teacher acknowledged this when he said, 'I'd make a point of not turning my back on them or not taking my eyes off them. I would say that eyes are the greatest controlling factor.' Another said, 'I keep alert. It's very tiring, but I keep an eye on them all the time. I can keep this attention by staring a bit rudely for the first two or three weeks.' This does not mean that a teacher should look around the class, searching for pupils to 'stare out', but simply that sustained eye contact is an expression of confidence and control.

Another factor suggesting status difference is orientation. Robertson (1989) suggests that the greater the status difference between two people, the more likely it is that the subordinate will face the superior. Although it is not always possible during physical education lessons, teachers usually expect pupils to face them when they are talking (it is probably unreasonable to expect a pupil hanging from the wall bars to face the teacher giving instruction!). If a pupil were to turn or look away in this situation, it would normally be understood as a sign of lack of respect or disengagement from the activity. There is less of a need for teachers to face pupils and, indeed, it is impossible for them to do so when dealing with a large group. However, turning to face a pupil directly is appropriate when that individual is singled out for a personal comment or a reprimand.

It is especially important for pupils to face the teacher when an explanation or set induction is being given. It is a fairly simple way of establishing attention, and can also make it easier for the teacher to judge if some pupils fail to understand the task presented to them. Different teachers have their own phrases and, especially with younger children, it is worth using a repeated phrase to request attention: 'Equipment down, looking at me'; 'Stop, look and listen'; and so on.

Finally, the use of territory and space can accurately convey authority. Unlike classroom work, most physical education lessons involve a fluid, ever-changing space. However, there are times when a deliberate movement by the teacher into a pupil's personal space can be a powerful tool. In fact, research suggests that moving closer to pupils at work can improve both behaviour and overall performance of tasks.

Task 3.5

The following is a very useful experiment (adapted from Jacobson, 1983), which can increase your awareness of the use of voice and body language in communication. It can also be fun!

- *Step 1* Choose a person from any walk of life whom you recognize as a very good communicator. It might be a comedian, a politician or an actor. It is best if this person appears on television, as you can video and re-watch him or her.
- *Step 2* Watch this person a number of times, noticing features of his or her physical behaviour. For example, you might make note of the following:
  - unusual postures;
  - specific hand movements;
  - characteristic facial expressions;
  - walking patterns.

  This can be aided by turning off the volume on the television.
- *Step 3* Listen for distinctive features in the person's voice, such as:
  - the use of particular phrases;

– voice quality, pitch and tone;
– volume and inflection;
– speed and tempo of speech.
This step can be made easier by turning away from the screen or closing your eyes whilst listening.

- *Step 4* Try to identify patterns of these sights and sounds. Is a particular gesture or intonation used at certain times and not others? Is a physical behaviour always accompanied by a vocal feature? Some people change the pitch of a word they wish to emphasize, or make a gesture when they have finished speaking.
- *Step 5* Once you have identified actions, sounds and patterns, try to copy them. Stand in front of a mirror, and try to duplicate the specific features of the physical behaviour and voice of the chosen individual. This should not be done solemnly, but with a sense of play and exploration. The aim is not to open up a new career as an impersonator, but simply to increase your awareness of the different ways that skilled communicators put across their message through the effective use of voice and body language.

Teachers not only need to be aware of their own body language; they also need to be able to read clues from that of the pupils'. Specifically, it is useful to monitor gesture and movement associated with misbehaviour. Children engaged in inappropriate behaviour often look towards the teacher in a furtive manner, or look around the area in search of allies. The noise level in the area may also increase. Brown (1975) suggests some other signals that can aid the teacher in monitoring a class:

- *Posture*. Are pupils turned towards or away from the object of the lesson?
- *Head orientation*. Are pupils looking at or away from the object of the lesson?
- *Faces*. Do students look sleepy or awake? Do they look withdrawn or involved? Interested or uninterested?
- *Activities*. Are they working on something related to the lesson or are they attending to something else? Where they are talking to their fellow students are their discussions task-orientated?

High hopes

One aspect of teaching that has received a great deal of attention from researchers is related to teacher expectations of pupils' abilities and behaviours. A number of writers have proposed that teachers' attitudes and expectations towards their pupils can have a considerable effect upon teachers' behaviour towards those pupils, and that this in turn influences the pupils' behaviours. Rink (1993: 47) refers to these as 'expectancy effects', which, she says, deal with the relationship between teacher expectations for pupil behaviour, the characteristics of the pupil and the actual achievement of the pupil.

Numerous studies have suggested that pupils of different levels of achievement are treated in different ways by teachers in terms of the frequency and quality of the contacts between them (Cohen, Manion and Morrison, 1996). High achievers seem to be given more opportunities to respond to teachers' questions and more time to answer than low achievers. They are also allowed to ask more questions themselves, and are offered more praise from teachers.

Some teachers' expectations about pupil achievement can be influenced by factors that have little or nothing to do with ability. Teachers' expectations about pupils' achievement is largely determined by their perception of pupil effort, and sometimes by how well pupils behave. These expectations can have both indirect and direct effects on pupils' learning. Indirectly, low teacher expectation may lead some pupils to modify their perception of their own ability, which may influence the goals they set themselves and the standards with which they are satisfied. More directly, well-meaning teachers may actually restrict the learning opportunities they offer some pupils. Teacher expectations and help may also be related to certain characteristics of pupils. Evidence suggests that high achievers and boys receive more teacher attention than low achievers and girls. Teachers also give less time and attention to pupils they believe to have poor motivation.

Mortimore and his colleagues (1994) carried out a review of the literature on teacher expectations related to specific groups. They identified some significant patterns. For example, pupils from non-manual backgrounds were rated as of a higher ability than pupils from manual backgrounds, even after account had been taken of their attainment. Boys generally receive a greater amount of criticism and neutral comments than girls, from both male and female teachers. Girls receive significantly more praise. However, teachers tend to rate boys slightly more favourably than girls in terms of ability, even after account has been taken of attainment.

Perhaps the most important step in dealing with expectancy effects is for teachers to be aware of them. There is an interesting paradoxical effect that can arise when teachers deliberately target specific groups for attention, even if they have previously been somewhat marginalized. Mortimore and his colleagues suggest that, by their willingness to single out some groups, teachers may be indicating lower academic expectations.

Task 3.6

- Reflect upon your own assumptions regarding ability of pupils from different groups. Do you hold any expectations that might influence the way you interact with pupils?
- Discuss this matter with your mentor.
- Ask your mentor or a colleague to observe a lesson you are teaching. The mentor should pay particular attention to the amount of time you spend with different groups – more and less able, boys and girls, and so on. What does the observation show?

On-task behaviour

'Practice time is perhaps the most critical element in the learning of a motor skill or the development of fitness' (Rink, 1993: 65).

An important skill for new teachers to develop involves the monitoring of pupils' involvement in their work, and correction when they deviate from it. Even in classes in which all pupils appear to be active and well behaved, there may be some who are doing something other than the task that has been set, perhaps because that task is seen as too easy or too challenging, or of no interest. Other pupils become 'competent bystanders' (Siedentop, 1991), that is, they may appear co-operative and responsive but subtly avoid full participation in the activities prescribed. Some teachers seem content to tolerate such behaviour, so long as pupils appear physically active and well behaved. This attitude, sometimes called the 'busy, happy and good' syndrome (Placek, 1983), is deceptively appealing but ultimately inadequate, since it places pupils' learning in a position of incidental importance behind a superficial image of activity.

'On-task behaviour' refers to pupils' involvement in a task as set by the teacher. A related concept is 'academic learning time' (ALT), which is 'the amount of time a student spends on an academic task he/she can perform with high success. The more ALT a student accumulates, the more the student is learning' (Fisher *et al*, 1980: 8). Whether the implicit equation of amount of time on-task and amount of learning taking place is accepted or not, it is difficult to deny that pupils are more likely to be working towards the learning objectives of a lesson if they are attending to the activities designed to facilitate their achievement of them. Therefore, the concepts of on-task behaviour and academic learning time are of some significance to the teacher.

Physical education researchers have taken up the idea of ALT, and developed an observation tool to record learning time in physical education lessons – ALT-PE (see

Mawer, 1995, for an accessible summary). Generally speaking, findings have indicated a surprisingly low amount of time in lessons during which pupils were actually actively involved in practising the skills and activities planned for them. Metzler (1989), for example, concluded that only about 10–20 per cent of total lesson time could be accurately seen as contributing to learning objectives. Other studies (reported in Mawer, 1995) found that less than 15 per cent of lesson time was taken up with pupils engaged in tasks of an appropriate level of difficulty, whilst a third of the time was spent 'waiting'. Studies suggesting that pupils taught by more experienced physical education teachers engage in greater amounts of learning time led Silverman (1991: 356) to conclude: 'Overwhelming evidence indicates that the amount of time students spend practising… at an appropriate or successful level is positively related to student achievement and that inappropriate or unsuccessful practice is negatively related to achievement.'

The box below describes a simple exercise in which an observer records the amount of on-task activity during a lesson. There are various ways of carrying out this exercise, but perhaps the easiest is for a colleague or mentor to observe and the less experienced teacher to teach the lesson.

On-task behaviour observation sheet

Purpose

This observation sheet is a flexible way of indicating the amount of on-task behaviour of pupils during a physical education lesson. It is not a formal measure, but simply a way of providing information to the teacher of the lesson regarding pupil activity during a specified lesson. It is intended as a focus of discussion with the observer, who should be a colleague.

Preparation

The observer will need: a stopwatch, a clipboard, an observation sheet and a pencil.

Procedure

1   The observer should sit away from the class, in an unobtrusive part of the physical education area. S/he should have a clear view of the whole area. If possible, the observer should be present in the area *before* the class enters.

2. Record the following at the start of the lesson:
   - time introduction started;
   - time activities began.
3. Once the class begins practical activities, randomly select three pupils. If they are organized into groups or pairs, choose pupils from different groups, or from different zones of the area.
4. Continually scan the *whole class*, making sure that the selected individuals are unaware that they are being observed.
5. Using the simple key on the sheet, record the behaviour of each of the selected pupils in consistent order every 15 seconds on the sheet, adding a brief comment if necessary (for example, if off task, the type of behaviour exhibited; if working in a group, the names of the other pupils; if performing, the level of success, and so on). Each pupil is recorded once every minute.
6. The periods of observation should be spaced as follows for a one-hour lesson (adapted as necessary for different length lessons):
   - Period 1: first 10 minutes of activity;
   - Period 2: from 25th to 35th minute;
   - Period 3: final 10 minutes.
7. The key indicates five behaviours (these can be changed to meet the needs of the teacher):
   - 'on task': pupil is actively engaged in task set by teacher;
   - 'near task': pupil is engaged in a task that resembles the set task, but has been modified/simplified in some way;
   - 'off task': pupil is not engaging in the task set by the teacher, nor speaking to the teacher or waiting to take a turn;
   - 'teacher attending': the teacher is speaking, either to the individual or the group/class;
   - 'waiting': pupil is waiting to take a turn or use a specific piece of equipment, as directed by teacher.
8. At the end of the lesson, feed back observations to teacher.

An example of an on-task behaviour observation sheet is given in Figure 3.2.

Kounin (1970) summarized the qualities of teachers that are positively related to pupil involvement in appropriate activities and to freedom from misbehaviour:

- *with-it-ness* – having 'eyes in the back of the head';
- *overlapping* – being able to do more than one thing at once, such as dealing with an individual whilst continuing to scan the rest of the class;
- *smoothness* – keeping children at work, by not interrupting when not necessary or not switching between tasks abruptly or unexpectedly;

On-task Behaviour Observation Sheet

Date: Lesson Theme:
Teacher: Observer:
Time Intro Started: Time Activity Started:

Key: = ✓ on task   ? = near task   𝑋 = off task   T = teacher attending   W = waiting

1 COMMENTS	2 COMMENTS	3 COMMENTS	4 COMMENTS

END OF PERIOD 1

END OF PERIOD 2

Figure 3.2   On-task behaviour observation sheet

- *overdwelling* – avoiding staying with an activity longer than necessary;
- *momentum* – freedom from 'slowdowns'.

One skill that can make a very valuable contribution to a teacher's awareness during a lesson is *scanning*. Experienced teachers frequently take time to look around the whole area to ensure that all pupils are appropriately engaged in their activities. Scanning is also useful in helping teachers to spot likely causes of future disturbance or difficulty, allowing them to 'nip it in the bud'. After a while, scanning becomes habitual, but in the early stages it requires conscious attention and practice.

An important factor within physical education lessons is the teacher's position within the area. A teacher standing in the middle of an area is not going to be able to scan the whole class (see Figure 3.3).

This position should be avoided whenever possible. Even when dealing with a specific group or individual, it is possible to be located so as to continue to scan the rest of the class, as is illustrated in Figure 3.4.

Effective teachers are not only aware of what is going on in their lessons, but they also use a range of techniques to ensure that pupils remain on task. Kounin (1970) used the phrase 'signal continuity' to refer to strategies that keep pupils 'on their toes' without causing unnecessary disruption to the lesson. This might involve the use of eye contact, focused questioning or moving near to pupils who are becoming off task. The virtue of these approaches is that they do not stop the rest of the class from working and learning, as might a loud verbal reprimand.

There is also a positive side to the awareness and monitoring of pupil behaviour. A teacher who is 'with it' is better able to spot good performance, and recognition of their high-quality work can be very motivating for pupils. Drawing attention to positive features of one group's work has the added benefit of reminding others of what is expected from them (Mawer, 1995).

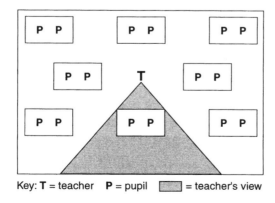

Key: **T** = teacher   **P** = pupil   ▨ = teacher's view

Figure 3.3   Inappropriate positioning of the teacher

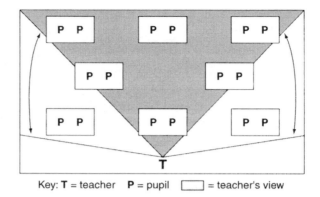

Key: **T** = teacher **P** = pupil ☐ = teacher's view

Figure 3.4   More appropriate positioning of the teacher (with scanning)

Task **3.7**

Whilst observing more experienced colleagues, take particular note of the strategies used to maintain on-task behaviour in pupils. Use the following labels (from Kounin, 1970) as foci for your observations:

- with-it-ness;
- overlapping;
- smoothness;
- overdwelling;
- momentum.

(See text for explanations of labels.)

Summary

Lesson climates should be positive, purposeful and characterized by appropriate interpersonal relationships. Many of the skills necessary for positive working environments in physical education lessons need practice, but their contributions to pupils' learning and the general tone of the lesson make the effort worth while. Key points to remember include:

- Successful lesson climates are purposeful, task-orientated, relaxed, warm, supportive and have a sense of order.
- The effective teacher expresses authority through words, tone of voice and body language.

- It is important to maintain high expectations of the pupils' standards of performance and behaviour.
- The more time pupils spend working on a task that is appropriate for their age, experience and ability, the greater is the likelihood of them learning and achieving.

Further reading

Mawer, M (1995) *The Effective Teaching of Physical Education*, Chapters 6 and 7, Longman, London

Rink, J E (1993) *Teaching Physical Education for Learning*, Chapter 7, Mosby, St Louis, MO

Siedentop, D (1991) *Developing Teaching Skills in Physical Education*, Mayfield, Mountain View, CA

4 Lesson organization and management

Introduction

Effective class organization and management are central elements in effective delivery of physical education lessons, and so play important roles in the promotion of effective pupil learning. It is well established that the more time pupils spend actively engaged in tasks offering an appropriate level of challenge, the greater will be their opportunities for learning, success and achievement. Class organization and management strategies are designed to maximize pupils' on-task behaviour, as part of an overall positive working environment.

It is important to recognize that the organization and management of physical education lessons are merely parts of a wider approach to teaching and learning, also discussed in other chapters in this book. Planning, teaching skills, control strategies and monitoring procedures are all elements that contribute to an effective, purposeful, positive learning climate, and none should be seen in isolation.

Objectives

By the end of this chapter you should:

- understand the importance of rules and routines in promoting learning;
- be aware of strategies for organizing time, pupils and space to maximize participation and learning;
- know the principles of safe practice in physical education lessons.

'Teachers are expected to be good classroom managers. Administrators often consider teachers who exert strong control to be their best teachers, while parents and the community expect students to be taught self-control. Likewise, students expect teachers to exert control and establish a positive learning environment' (Cruickshank, Bainer and Metcalf, 1995: 393).

Rules

Rules specify acceptable forms of behaviour before, during and after lessons. They play an important role in establishing the teacher's control and dominance in the lesson, and in clarifying expectations about the way lessons will take place. They also reflect the values of the teacher and the school. Perhaps the most fundamental value that ought to be promoted and reinforced throughout physical education is that of respect for oneself and others, and the rules ought to reflect this. Many of the general classroom rules will equally apply in physical education lessons, but may need to be adapted for the new context. Others will need to be introduced specifically for the peculiar learning environments in which physical education takes place.

A possible list of general rules for physical education lessons (from Lambirth and Bailey, 2000) might include:

- We listen when others are talking.
- We respect everyone in the class.
- We take care of equipment.
- We always try our best during PE lessons.
- We always do as the teacher asks.

Traditionally, schools have used too many rules, and have tended to emphasize punitive ones. The dangers of long, negative lists are that they are difficult to recall and follow, and they act as an obstacle to the maintenance of a positive working climate. Therefore, the teacher needs to consider limiting the number of rules presented to a class, especially when working with younger children. Cohen, Manion and Morrison (1996) suggest three criteria for selecting such a minimal list:

- relevance;
- meaningfulness;
- positiveness.

Relevance

Rules should contribute to pupils' learning and safety in lessons. To be relevant, they should be flexible, and may vary from context to context. Different activity areas have their own specific rules. They may also have different standards of behaviour, and the teacher will need to spend some time emphasizing the different applications of the rules. For example, acceptable noise level can vary considerably between swimming, outdoor activities and gymnastics.

Meaningfulness

Pupils are much more likely to recall and adhere to rules that seem meaningful and sensible to them than to a list of arbitrary commands. Rules are best that follow logically from the activity and are not entirely of the teacher's creation. Indeed, some have argued that rules operate most successfully when they have been negotiated with the pupils (Lambirth and Bailey, 2000). The opportunity for serious discussion about physical education rules is likely to vary between primary and secondary schools, and secondary teachers will have much less contact with a particular class through the week. Nevertheless, engaging pupils in the articulation of rules offers them a sense of ownership of those rules and a heightened sense of responsibility to conform to them.

Positiveness

A list of 'don't do' and 'no' rules should be avoided, whenever possible. Positive rules show pupils a goal to work towards, and are more purposeful than statements of things to avoid. Negative lists can also detract from the positive working climate. Statements like 'Don't talk when others are talking', 'No running at the side of the pool' and 'Don't damage equipment' can easily be rephrased in positive terms, without losing any meaning: 'Listen when others are talking'; 'Walk slowly and carefully at the side of the pool'; 'Take care of all of our equipment.'

Task 4.1

Each activity area has its own specific requirements and safety issues, and so may need its own set of rules. Compile a list of area-specific rules for each activity area. Remember to keep the lists brief (perhaps including only three or four points per area):

- gymnastics;
- games;
- dance;
- swimming;
- outdoor and adventurous activities;
- athletics.

Rules should be presented or negotiated from the very first meetings with a class. These early encounters are key periods for laying down expectations of behaviour, and set the scene for the coming year's working and learning (see Chapter 11 for a full discussion of this vital aspect of effective teaching).

The teacher needs to continue reinforcing the rules and expectations throughout the year, and especially once the novelty of a new teacher wears off. It is often during the second or third weeks of the first term that some pupils begin to test the teacher, to see if these standards are going to be enforced or not. Like many other forms of behaviour, adherence to rules requires repeated emphasis. This is best carried out at an appropriate moment, such as within the context in which it applies. So, emphasizing a rule related to the need for everyone to wait until all pupils have thrown their javelins and the teacher has given an express command to retrieve them is much better presented *before* pupils throw than afterwards!

In order to make rules as meaningful as possible for pupils, it may be worth while to use examples of good and bad practice. This is especially useful with younger children, for whom abstract ideas may be less comprehensible than concrete demonstrations. Another strategy is for rules to be displayed in prominent areas around the physical education area. For example, generic rules of behaviour in lessons can be posted where pupils line up before entering the gym, where everybody is going to see them. Posted rules can also be used for highly specific situations, such as the use of gymnastics apparatus or getting equipment from the PE store.

Routines

Routines are procedures for carrying out certain tasks that regularly occur. They form an essential element of good class management, and are among the very first things that teachers need to organize. Establishing routines enables the teacher to manage time most effectively during lessons and so maximize opportunities for learning. As with rules, the best routines are those that follow logically from the demands of the task, and for which pupils can see a purpose. Again, involving pupils in the planning of routines is a useful strategy, especially in the primary years. The great majority of pupils, like the teacher, want a smooth, well-managed session that promotes learning and participation.

There are numerous routines that contribute to successful physical education lessons. Not all are relevant in all situations, and should be adopted selectively. They relate to the aspects of the lesson presented in Task 4.2.

Task 4.2

These are some of the most common topics of routines in physical education lessons:

- changing;
- entering the physical education area;
- signals;
- giving instructions;
- organizing groups;
- distributing and returning equipment;
- use of space;
- ending the lesson and leaving the area.

Talk with your mentor about the routines used by physical education teachers in your school. Using the headings given above as a starting point, list the specific decisions that need to be made in the establishment of routines. For example, you may decide that signals need to be introduced and reinforced, such as 'Start', 'Stop when you have finished your task', 'Stop immediately' and 'Come to the teacher.'

Changing

In primary schools, changing usually takes place in the classroom; secondary school pupils usually have designated changing rooms. Changing is a potentially wasteful period of the physical education lesson, and it is important to establish strict expectations of behaviour and changing time early in the year. This is especially the case in secondary schools, where a teacher may not be able to supervise pupils of the opposite sex directly (some schools overcome this problem by making sure that male and female teachers' classes change simultaneously). Some teachers turn changing into a game, and challenge pupils to break their own class 'record'. This can work wonderfully to motivate younger children and, if combined with an expectation that the whole class is to work together, can encourage faster changers to help their slower peers. Procedures for collecting and storing jewellery and other valuables should be included in this routine, perhaps by designating one pupil to collect items and pass them to the teacher for safe storage.

Entering the physical education area

It is often the case that the first moments set the scene for the rest of the lesson. It is important, therefore, to establish routines in which pupils enter the area calmly, quietly and with order. Understandably, pupils may be excited at the thought of the lesson, but this needs to be controlled in the name of safety. When entering the area, pupils might be expected to sit in a designated location, such as on floor markings or on benches, or simply sit in a space. Older pupils can be taught to begin their own warm-up activities as they enter the area.

Signals

It is essential that pupils are familiar with and respond to signals to start and stop activities. It may also be useful to distinguish between a signal to stop when a task has been completed and to stop at once (the latter being necessary with a risk of injury). A whistle may be needed when teaching in large outside spaces. In enclosed areas, such as the gym or hall, the teacher's voice should be sufficient. Indeed, using a whistle indoors can actually increase the risk of injury, as its volume and piercing tone can easily distract pupils engaged in activities.

Giving instructions

If pupils cannot hear what the teacher is saying, they will not be a position to carry out the planned activities appropriately. It is important to insist upon absolute silence, and not to continue to speak until this has been achieved. Some teachers talk of 'playing the waiting game': they wait calmly until everyone in the class is looking and listening. This can be accompanied by taking a prominent position whilst looking pupils (or some pupils from different parts of the group) in the eye, and not proceeding until all comply. After a while the class will realize that it is much easier and less boring to do as the teacher asks.

Organizing groups and space

The important issue of organizing groups and space is discussed in detail later in this chapter.

Distributing and returning equipment

A particularly important issue relates to the safe and effective handling of large equipment (such as gymnastic apparatus), and this deserves systematic training by the teacher. Learning how to handle physical education equipment is an essential skill for pupils to acquire, and children of all ages can be taught to distribute and set up their equipment in a reasonable amount of time. However, this requires practice at the start of the year and reinforcement throughout. Ideally, there should be several access points to the equipment to avoid congestion or rushing for access and the associated risk of injury and misbehaviour.

Ending the lesson and leaving the area

Many physical education lessons involve pupils in vigorous or competitive activities, and these can result in the pupils becoming somewhat excited. Pupils should never leave the physical education area in such a state, and the teacher needs to plan tasks to get pupils' minds and bodies in an appropriate state. All physical education lessons should end with a cooling-down phase, perhaps including gentle, rhythmic movements or stretching. A few moments lying with eyes shut and breathing deeply can also help pupils calm down before leaving. This can be accompanied by simple visualization exercises (see Task 4.3). A game that works especially well with younger children is 'sleeping lions', in which the children lie quietly on the floor, breathing deeply and slowly, and the teacher whispers the names of quiet and still individuals, who then silently stand and line up ready to leave the area. The class leave when all pupils are quietly waiting in line.

Task 4.3

Visualization exercises can help pupils mentally practise skills and techniques they have used during a lesson, whilst effectively calming them down. One approach (among many) is given below:

1. At the end of the lesson, ask the pupils to lie quietly on their backs, on the floor (on a gym mat if necessary). Their arms and legs should not be crossed, and should extend naturally.
2. As you talk to the class, try to slow and lower the tone of your voice: 'Close your eyes. Try to focus upon your breath for a few moments, feeling it enter and leave your body. Now I want you to count your breaths in and out: count to 10; then start over again.'

3. 'Now imagine that you are looking at a big television screen. Are there any pictures or shapes on it? If there are, just enjoy what you are seeing for a moment. Are there any colours? Is there movement?'

4. 'Now try to clear the screen, and see another image appear on it. It is a picture of you doing [activity from preceding lesson]. You are doing it really well, the best you have ever done it. Look at the way you are moving. Perhaps you can become the director of the film. Perhaps you have a zoom camera that can zoom in on special parts of the action, and then move out to see the whole thing again. Perhaps you can switch from looking at yourself performing to seeing things through your own eyes. Again, you are doing the skill as well as you have ever done it. How does that feel?'

5. Allow the pupils to spend a minute or two visualizing themselves practising the skill.

6. 'When you are ready, slowly open your eyes. Enjoy the feeling of relaxation for a moment. Try stretching your arms up towards the ceiling. Now pull your knees to your chest and give them a gentle hug. When you are ready, slowly sit up. Now carefully stand up, and walk over to the door to line up.'

It is worth investing some time at the start of the year in establishing routines. This time will quickly be made up through the improved smooth running of the lessons. Early lessons can be planned with an emphasis upon laying down these foundations, and the intended learning objectives might stress pupils learning the routines more than the physical activities being carried out. It should also be acknowledged that early teaching of routines will not mean that teachers never need to deal with them again. Even after time has been spent during first encounters, pupils can still depart from routines unless they are reminded from time to time. This is particularly the case after a school holiday or other breaks from lessons.

Organizing time

A general principle of effective teaching is that the greater the amount of time pupils are engaged in activities, the more they may learn (Wragg, 1993). Of course, it is not always the case that a pupil who is busy is also learning, but it is certainly the case that a child who is not engaged with a task is less likely to be learning. So, the organization of time during lessons is an important factor in effective physical education teaching.

Ensuring that pupils spend a considerable proportion of lesson time engaged in challenging activities is a feature of positive class management, promoted throughout this book, and many of the principles of effective teaching discussed in other chapters are of equal relevance here. These principles include the following:

- Establish and reinforce efficient routines.
- Be clear of the expectations of behaviour, supported by workable control strategies.
- Delegate: use pupils to help set up and put away apparatus, and to distribute and collect equipment.
- Be brief and to the point in verbal instructions.
- Identify possible causes of disruption and plan strategies to address these, including transitions between phases of the lesson, queuing and waiting.
- Include expected time allocations of different activities in the lesson plan.
- Evaluate the appropriateness of your timings of phases of lessons.

The pace of the lesson refers to the time pupils spend on different tasks. Effective pacing is an important element in pupil learning and behaviour. However, it can be difficult to strike a balance between sufficient time on a task and appropriate progression through tasks. On the one hand, pupils should not spend so much time occupied on a specific activity that they become bored or engaged in mindless responses. The lesson should be brisk and purposeful, and lost time should be avoided. On the other hand, time is needed to properly practise certain skills and techniques, or for pupils to reflect upon their learning.

Like much else in teaching, a teacher's ability to pace a lesson improves with experience. The decision to continue with a task or to change to the next is largely based upon the teacher's observation and monitoring of pupil learning. Observations by colleagues or a mentor can be invaluable in gauging whether adequate or excessive time has been allowed for tasks.

One of the most commonly cited obstacles to effective pacing of lessons is excessive teacher talk, especially during introductions to lessons. Inexperienced teachers are particularly prone to orate for great periods of time, when pupils' learning would be better served by actually having a go at the activity. Fontana (1985) suggests that teachers should limit the amount of time they engage in continuous talk to no more than a minute and a half for each year of the average class age. In physical education lessons, this figure should be considered a *maximum total talk time*, which is the time teachers are talking and pupils are *not* actively engaged in tasks. So, for six-year-olds, the total time during the lesson that the teacher would talk to pupils would be nine minutes. For 10-, 14- and 18-year-olds, it would rise to a total of 15, 21 and 27 minutes respectively. The rest of the lesson ought to be taken up with meaningful, challenging learning tasks.

Organizing groups

The importance and value of working with others in physical education has been repeatedly emphasized by National Curriculum documents. Almost all work in physical education is carried out with other people, and the great potential for co-operative learning is one of the distinguishing features of the subject. Moreover, as Fisher (1995) points out, an important factor in working in groups is that it imposes intellectual as well as social challenges on pupils.

Many physical education activities would simply not be possible unless pupils were organized into groups. However, there are wider benefits to pupils of working in groups. For example, it:

- encourages co-operation;
- enables pupils to learn from one another;
- encourages the involvement of all pupils;
- removes the stigma of failure from pupils;
- enables pupils to work at their own pace;
- enables pupils to respect others' strengths and weaknesses;
- affords access to scarce equipment;
- encourages joint decision making;
- focuses on processes as well as products;
- is particularly effective for problem-solving activities;
- encourages pupils to engage in the problem of disagreement.

(Adapted from Cohen, Manion and Morrison, 1996.)

These benefits do not necessarily come to pupils simply through them being arranged into groups. Teachers need to devote time to training pupils to work effectively with others, through developing their skills of speaking, listening, collaborating and taking turns. They also need to consider appropriate group size for an activity, the types of groups within the lesson and procedures for arranging pupils into groups.

Group size

To a large extent, the size of groups in which pupils work will be determined by the type of activity they are carrying out. However, there are other factors that need to be taken into consideration when planning, such as availability of equipment and space, and wider educational goals. Some games like tennis and badminton will normally suggest pupils working in pairs or fours, but there may be benefit from practising certain skills individually (for example, practising a new technique alone in the first instance) or in larger groups (a whole-class warming-up game). There are also likely to be 'spare' players when dividing a class into groups (a class of 29 might be broken up into six groups of four, and one group of five players), who need to be active and engaged in the lesson throughout.

In games situations, it is often a useful strategy for players to practise skills initially alone or in pairs, and to develop progressively to working in larger and more complex groups. This progression might take place during the lesson, or over a series of lessons. Decisions regarding group size are often a compromise between two competing factors. On the one hand, larger groups normally mean greater social and strategic challenge. On the other hand, smaller groups promote greater opportunity for participation and physical activity.

Younger children in particular benefit from working with small groups. Small-sided activities offer a solution to the inherent complexity of much of the physical education curriculum. By the end of Key Stage 1, for example, pupils are ready to take part in rule-governed games, but many will still be challenged by quite complex social questions – What is my role? What are their roles? What are they likely to do? How will they respond to my actions? (Lee, 1993) – which can lead to confusion. Small-sided tasks reduce the variables, so that children are better able to develop an understanding of an activity's requirements. By gradually developing work in pairs, threes and fours, and by offering the chance to play in different positions, teachers can introduce children into the rules and roles of an activity in a way that is manageable, yet challenging (Bailey, 1999b).

Kagan (1988) introduces another element to the debate, by arguing that certain groupings favour and others hinder pupils' opportunities for interaction. This may be less significant in activities that focus upon skill performance, but does seem to be relevant in the numerous tasks requiring social interaction and communication, such as problem solving, pupil planning and evaluation. Consider the diagrams in Figure 4.1.

Kagan (1988) pointed out that the number of pupils in a group will determine the number of lines of communication. He claims that groups of four are ideal, since

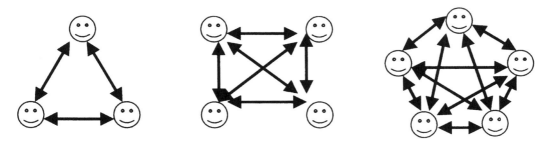

Figure 4.1   Lines of communication in groups of three, four and five pupils (adapted from Bennett and Dunne, 1994)

three often become a pair and a spare. Also, note from Figure 4.1 that the number of possible lines of communication doubles when changing from threes to fours (from three to six lines), which increases the opportunity for social learning. Groups of five often leave a pupil out, and larger groups can reduce the time for individual participation.

Types of groups

Another important issue regarding grouping concerns the criteria by which groups are formed. Rink (1993: 70) warns that 'grouping is a powerful tool that a teacher can use to influence the learning process', so it ought not to be left to chance. Criteria for organizing groups include:

- ability;
- gender;
- developmental;
- friendship;
- random.

When given the choice, pupils will often group themselves in generally similar *ability* groups in physical education lessons (Rink, 1993). Working with peers of similar ability can challenge and stimulate pupils, and can also help reduce the stress some feel when working alongside much more able peers. As was discussed in Chapter 2, negative comparison of physical competence can be very harmful to children's social relations and self-esteem, so activities with a strong competitive element might suggest grouping by ability. Some authors suggest that ability grouping is divisive and harmful to pupils' self-esteem, especially if used regularly (eg Pollard and Tann, 1993). However, a great deal depends on the sensitivity of teachers and their ability to make each group feel valued and deserving of attention.

The question of *gender* grouping presents the teacher with something of an ethical dilemma, especially in the secondary school. There is little doubt that boys and girls need to learn to communicate and work together, and that physical education lessons can act as powerful media in which they can learn these skills. It is also the case that grouping by gender can convey certain messages to the class, especially if the teacher has different expectations of the different groups. However, it is not the case that mixed-sex teaching will equate to equal opportunities (Talbot, 1996), and there is a considerable amount of research suggesting that many girls, especially in secondary school, do not want mixed-sex physical education. Scraton (1993) identifies a number of reasons why mixed-sex grouping has often failed to be successful: boys dominate lessons, both verbally and physically; they take up more of the teacher's time; and they often marginalize girls to only occasional involvement as participants unless the girls are exceptionally skilful. She concludes that interaction between pupils within mixed settings 'remains single-sex unless there is a positive intervention by the teacher' (Scraton, 1993: 143–44). This last point is the key: teachers have to be especially careful to manage activities and foster positive working relationships between boys and girls, or run the risk of blocking girls' learning and damaging their enthusiasm for physical education. Recent research by the Institute of Youth Sport (2000) has found that well-planned and taught mixed-sex physical education lessons can be positive and worthwhile experiences for all pupils, and can benefit both girls *and* boys.

In any Key Stage 2 or Key Stage 3 class, there is likely to be a mix of pre-pubescent, pubescent and post-pubescent pupils, and consequently there will be wide variations in physique and physical ability (see Bailey, 2000a). Not all activities will be suitable for all pupils with these classes, so there may be times when *developmental* groups are useful, each working on differentiated tasks.

Most people like to work with their friends, and *friendship* groups can be a popular option. However, it is important for the teacher to bear a few points in mind when considering such groupings: some friends are well suited for chatting but not working; most friendship groups are single-sex; and some children may be left out. The important point, again, is sensitive handling by the teacher to avoid problems.

Sometimes the make-up of groups makes no difference for the planned activity, and the teacher can opt for *random* groupings. There are numerous ways of randomly forming teams, and it is worth experimenting with different strategies and finding ones that work for you. One strategy that is not recommended is that of picking 'captains', who proceed to pick their teams, starting with their friends and the most able players, and leaving the less able to last, dejected and humiliated.

Some methods for arranging pupils into groups are outlined in the box below.

- 'The Number Game' – pupils move around the area individually, the teacher calls out a number and the pupils form groups of that size. Pupils should form groups quietly and without physically pulling friends into their group! This can be made into a competition: 'Which group is ready first?' Additional rules can be added, like 'Each group must have at least one boy and one girl in it.'
- A variation follows on from the Number Game: the pupils number off, eg 1 to 4. All the '1's form together, all the '2's and so on.
- Group according to the colour of eyes, or letters of the alphabet, or birthdays.
- After a whole-class warm-up activity, pupils sit in a space and the teacher divides up the area to form groups.

Task 4.4

Discuss strategies for forming groups with colleagues, and extend the list in the box above.

Organizing space

The effective use of space is an important factor in successful physical education lessons. Activities involve pupils in moving around the area, often at speed or with projectiles, so the teacher needs to think carefully about ways of using the limited space available in such a way as promotes participation and safety.

Teachers need to define the area of the physical education area in which work will take place, and they may also need to break up that space into smaller zones for groups or specific tasks (Rink, 1993). Sometimes, there are natural boundaries (such as in a swimming pool or the walls of a gym), but otherwise it is necessary to define clearly the available playing area to pupils. Younger children can easily forget the boundaries in the excitement of a game, and need reminding from time to time, especially if they are working in an area where obstacles are surrounding the physical education area. Warm-up games can easily be adapted to reinforce boundaries (eg pupils travel around the designated area, bending down to touch the edge of the area when they reach it; this can be extended to great effect by pretending that the boundary is an 'electric fence', so the pupils have to make a buzzing noise when they reach the edge of the area).

Different activities require different amounts of space. For example, gymnastics involves a fixed area, but one in which space is of a premium. In this case, it is worth the teacher planning in some detail (drawn on the reverse of the lesson plan) how the area will be utilized. Similarly, racket games use limited net space, and too closely packed groups can present a safety problem. At the other extreme are striking and fielding games played on a field. If pupils are not restricted in their available playing space, balls can easily be lost and time wasted. In this context, marking off zones for targeting strikes can be helpful, as can using walls for hitting balls against.

Markers and cones are widely available in schools, and offer easy and highly effective ways of breaking up a large area into smaller parts. This might be necessary to ensure that all pupils have a fair amount of space or to separate groups for safety purposes. Reducing the amount of space to perform skills can also increase the complexity of the task, as pupils have less time and space to manoeuvre and react to other players' actions. Figure 4.2 suggests a number of different approaches to using space in physical education lessons.

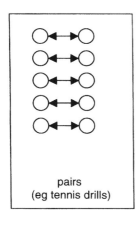

pairs
(eg tennis drills)

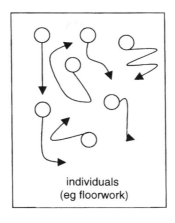

individuals
(eg floorwork)

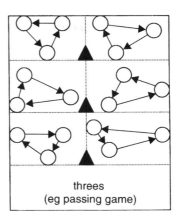

threes
(eg passing game)

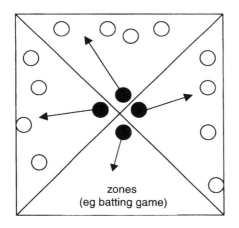

zones
(eg batting game)

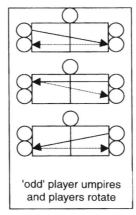

'odd' player umpires
and players rotate

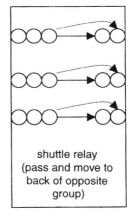

shuttle relay
(pass and move to
back of opposite
group)

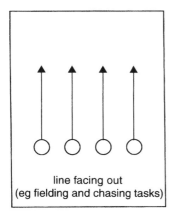

line facing out
(eg fielding and chasing tasks)

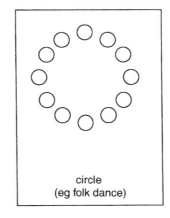

circle
(eg folk dance)

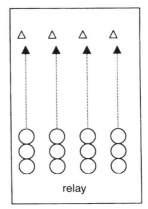

relay

Figure 4.2 Organization of groups and space

Organizing equipment

Related to the use of space is the organization of equipment, and both make significant contributions to pupils' levels of activity and engagement during lessons. Ideally, all classes would have access to all of the equipment they needed, but in reality schools have limited budgets. Primary teachers may find that there is insufficient equipment for each pupil to have their ball or racket or mat. So a compromise between what is desirable and what is achievable is necessary. The sensible use of group work is one approach to making the most of the equipment. Whatever the shortcomings of supplies, it is important to ensure that all available equipment is used, and thorough preparation and planning of lessons will help prevent unexpected shortages. Thorough planning is also needed to ensure that transitions between different activities do not result in losing pace and momentum, as pupils change and change again their equipment.

If possible and relevant, pupils should be given some choice of the equipment they are using. Different individuals have different learning needs, and access to a variety of sizes and shapes of equipment can support their learning (see Chapter 7). By offering them choice, pupils are also engaged more actively in their own learning, as they are forced to ask themselves, 'What is the most appropriate equipment to use in this situation?'

There are many different ways of distributing equipment to pupils. Perhaps the worst is to place it all in one corner of the area and invite the pupils to help themselves. Over 30 children running headlong into a small space is the stuff of which disasters are made! Less hazardous approaches include asking one member of each group to get the equipment for the others, or distributing the equipment for the lesson in clusters around the outside of the physical education area (making sure that it doesn't cause a safety problem by interfering with pupils' movement around the area) and allowing groups to access the nearest supply (see Figure 4.3).

Safe practice

'The first thing a teacher always needs to determine is whether the learning environment is a safe one. Safety takes precedence over all other concerns' (Rink, 1993: 148).

A moment's thought will reveal the many different contexts within physical education lessons where injury to pupils might occur. Pupils run and jump at speed, often in a restricted area; they throw and strike objects; they change direc-

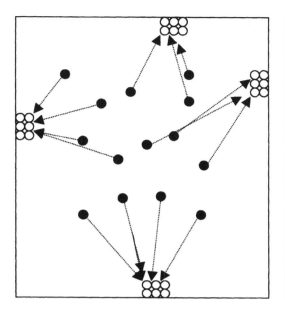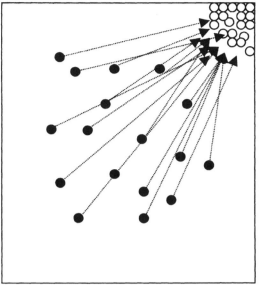

Figure 4.3 Safe (left) and unsafe ways of distributing equipment

tions and evade. Accidents are not inevitable, but their threat presents a constant warning for teachers to plan and deliver lessons with safety at the forefront.

It is especially important at the start of one's teaching career to make planning for safety explicit, and lesson plans should always make some reference to relevant points. By being aware of potential dangers and paying attention to them throughout the lesson, the risk of accident is greatly minimized. With time, many of these procedures will become habitual, but the teacher will still need to be reminded of good practice, and this is best done through proper lesson planning.

Teachers have a 'duty of care' for the safety of their pupils. According to BAALPE (1995), the level of care exhibited by teachers should be even greater than that of parents, since teachers are assumed to know more about children's propensities. Unfortunately, many non-specialist trainee teachers receive very limited physical education training, and this may mean that they lack the confidence and competence to make sound judgements regarding safety in all activity areas. Expertise can be enhanced through continued professional development. However, even qualified teachers should not attempt to teach an activity above their present level of competence (Macfadyen, 2000b).

The many, varied and specific situations that arise in physical education mean that safety is a vast subject, one beyond the remit of this book. Readers are strongly encouraged to turn to *Safe Practice in Physical Education*, published by the British Association of Advisers and Lecturers in Physical Education (BAALPE, 1995), which is available in most schools and university libraries. It offers a clear and thorough treatment of the main issues, including reference to specific sports and activities.

Task 4.5

All schools have health and safety documents, and there should also be safety guidance within physical education policy documentation. Ask to see your school's safety documentation, and discuss it with your mentor or colleagues. Consult the generic sections of *Safe Practice in Physical Education* (BAALPE, 1995). Also, familiarize yourself with the school's accident and emergency procedures.

Start to compile a list of safety points for each of the activities you are going to teach. Spend some time doing this, and show your list to your mentor. What are the best ways of ensuring these points are put into practice during your lessons – class rules, teacher preparation, routines?

Make sure your lesson plans contain information on safety issues in all of your lessons.

This section will merely highlight main areas of consideration, especially those of relevance to the trainee or newly qualified teacher.

Indoor physical education areas

- Before the class enters the area, inspect the floor for dirt, liquid or damage. Also, check for wet, over-polished or otherwise slippery floors.
- Push obstacles, such as chairs, tables and pianos, away from the area in which pupils will be moving.
- Never allow pupils to work just in socks or tights.
- Check all gymnastic equipment before pupils use it.
- Ensure pupils know how to carry heavy equipment safely.
- When pupils set up gymnastic apparatus, follow a three-part checking protocol (Macfadyen, 2000b):
  - Teacher checks equipment has been correctly positioned and that each piece occupies sufficient space for pupils to move on to, over and off without risk of collision or interference with other pupils.
  - Check that the apparatus is stable, that it has been properly assembled and that any pins or bolts have been securely fastened.
  - Check the equipment for damage, splinters and loose fastenings.

- On no account should improvised equipment, such as dining tables and stage blocks, be used in physical education lessons.
- Make sure you know where the first-aid kit is stored, and the school policy and procedures for administering first aid.

Outdoor areas

- If the playing fields are away from the school, establish strict routines for walking to and from them, especially if roads need to be crossed.
- Make sure you know where the first-aid kit is stored.
- Make sure that surfaces are even, and that there are no broken or loose areas of tarmac.
- Frost, rain, dew or falling leaves can all make surfaces dangerous.
- Establish rules and routines for retrieving lost equipment, especially when balls go on to roads.
- A sweep search of the field should be carried out before the lesson. Look for holes, glass and other hazards.
- Clarify boundaries for the lesson with pupils.

Clothing, jewellery and hair

- Jewellery and physical education do not mix. There is no place for jewellery in any circumstances, and it should be removed before lessons.
- Children have a greater sensitivity to extremes of heat and cold than adults. They should wear sufficient layers in cold weather to keep them warm, and loose, lightweight clothing in hot temperatures. Pupils should wear long sleeves, hats and sun cream in very sunny weather.
- Shoes should be appropriate for the task. Thick-soled trainers are not suitable for gymnastics. Flimsy plimsolls should not be worn on the playing field.
- Children usually have greater control and balance in bare feet during gymnastics and dance lessons.
- Despite the latest fashions, training shoelaces should be securely tied up.
- Long hair should be securely tied back.

Working with pupils

- It is vital to know if any pupils have special needs or medical conditions.
- Pupils with asthma should have their inhalers to hand, in case of an attack.
- Always start the lesson with a warm-up, and finish with a calming cool-down.
- The teacher should be positioned to see all pupils. Continuously scan the class for potential problems.
- Engage pupils in safety procedures. Knowing about the rules and routines of physical education is an important aspect of pupils' initiation into the subject.
- Report any injury to the designated person in the school. Note the incident in the school accident book.
- Accidents are less likely to happen if pupils appreciate possible risks and the importance of safe practice.

Summary

Lesson organization and management provide a foundation for effective, enjoyable and safe learning. This chapter has presented a range of strategies to facilitate good, safe practice. Key points to remember include:

- Safety is always the priority in physical education lessons.
- Establish and reinforce workable rules and routines.
- Plan the organization of time to encourage maximum participation in pairs.
- Different group types meet different purposes, and should be used selectively and sensitively.
- The use and organization of available space should be planned to facilitate safe and effective participation and learning.

Further reading

BAALPE (1999) *Safe Practice in Physical Education*, BAALPE, Dudley

Dean, J (1996) *Beginning to Teach in the Secondary School*, Chapters 6 and 7, Open University Press, Buckingham

Institute of Youth Sport (2000) *Towards Girl-Friendly Physical Education: The Nike/YST Girls In Sport partnership project (final report)*, IYS, Loughborough

Macfadyen, T M (2000) Creating a safe learning environment in physical education, in *Teaching Physical Education 5–11*, ed R P Bailey and T M Macfadyen, Continuum, London

5 Teaching skills

Introduction

Teachers need many different skills to promote pupil learning, participation and achievement. Some of these skills have already been discussed in the contexts of the planning and management of lessons. This chapter takes a narrower focus, by considering the specific strategies that form the teacher's 'toolkit', such as giving instructions, questioning, explaining and demonstrating. There is considerable evidence showing that good teachers are able to draw upon a wide range of teaching skills and styles, and it is essential that trainee and newly qualified teachers make every effort to develop their repertoire. Simply stated, the greater the variety of skills at your disposal, the better you will be able to meet the different challenges that will arise in physical education lessons.

Objectives

By the end of this chapter you should:

- be aware of a range of strategies for presenting information and instructions to pupils;
- be familiar with the key principles of questioning, explaining, demonstrating and intervening;
- understand the ways in which different teaching skills can support pupil learning.

Giving instructions

In order to maximize learning in physical education lessons and to minimize the likelihood of inappropriate behaviour, it is important that pupils have a clear idea of the activities they are being asked to do. Teacher talk should be concise and to the point, to allow pupils maximum time to engage in the activities. However, there is a danger of rushing through instructions, and this can easily result in pupils feeling unsure of the tasks in which they are expected to engage. The little time saved in giving overly brief instructions can be lost through frequent queries and requests for clarification from bewildered pupils.

There is little point in giving instructions to pupils who are not listening, so ensuring that all pupils are silent and attentive to the teacher is fundamental. This is an obvious but frequently overlooked point, and bears repeating: the teacher should not begin speaking until everyone is paying attention. Inexperienced teachers sometimes try to talk over chatting pupils, but this is usually unsuccessful, and can undermine the teacher's sense of authority. Factors that can interfere with attention in physical education lessons include:

- speaking;
- handling equipment;
- being distracted by events elsewhere in the area;
- excitement caused by previous or coming activity.

It is useful to develop a familiar phrase to gain attention. Through its repetition, pupils become conditioned to stop whatever they are doing and listen to the coming instructions. The phrase should be short and to the point, such as 'Stop, look and listen' or 'Equipment down, no noise and looking at me.'

The tone in which instructions are given is important, and teachers should be careful not to come across as either aggressive or indecisive. Barking orders to pupils, like a sergeant major to army recruits, induces fear and resistance. The opposite approach – 'I'd like you to get into groups, if that's OK with you' – comes across as weak and ineffectual. Pupils like their teachers to be in control of the lesson, whilst also treating them with respect. Marland (1975) captures this balance by suggesting that teachers aim for *firm warmth* or a *warm firmness*.

The simple act of listening to the teacher does not necessarily translate to pupils understanding what they are being asked to do. Some pupils find the language used in schools inaccessible. Others are confused by the complexity of the concepts involved. Williams (1996a: 56–57) warns that 'by the time they reach Key Stage 3 some pupils have given up hope of understanding what has been said and rely on watching other pupils and copying'. She goes on to suggest that 'what has been interpreted as misbehaviour and constant off-task behaviour can actually be a result of never understanding the task in the first place'.

Task 5.1

Working alongside a colleague or your mentor, give instructions for a task to the class and set them off to work. Then, while your colleague supervises the lesson, spend a few minutes with each group. Ask them to explain to you what they have been asked to do. Encourage them to offer their own interpretations of the instructions.

You may be quite surprised with the results of your informal survey. Many pupils who do not understand instructions are too embarrassed to ask for help, which only adds to their confusion.

Discuss strategies for sensitively identifying and handling pupil misunderstanding with your mentor.

The clarity of instructions can be improved by including reference to the points needing to be addressed in lesson plans. Difficult content might warrant word-for-word planning. At the very least, it is important to check understanding before sending pupils off to work. An idiosyncrasy of children seems to be that very few will admit incomprehension when asked, 'Does everyone understand?' But many more are likely to raise their hands when the question is rephrased negatively: 'Is there anyone who *does not understand*?'

A specific form of instruction is sometimes labelled 'set induction'. This refers to the introductory input of a unit of work, lesson or activity, during which the teacher focuses pupils' attention on what is going to be learnt or done. Although this phase should not be protracted, it does seem to be the case that a well-planned and delivered set induction will have a strong influence on pupils' learning outcomes.

There are four main functions of set induction (based on Perrott, 1982), which are illustrated in Table 5.1 with examples from physical education lessons.

Explanations

Many of the elements of effective instructions also apply to explanations, such as those related to conciseness, comprehension and clarity. Clarity is an especially important quality of explanations, and Perrott (1982) summarizes research findings indicating that clarity of explanation can exert considerable influence on effective teaching. She identifies three main elements that contribute to effectiveness in explanations:

Table 5.1   Functions of set induction in physical education lessons

Function	Examples
focusing learners' attention on what is going to be learnt by gaining their interest	– playing the music with which pupils will later be creating dances – playing a small-sided game as a way of creating a context for later skill practice
acting as a means of transition from tasks, concepts or material already experienced to new content about to be introduced	'Do you remember when we practised throwing in cricket? Can you tell me the main points to remember?' [Answers.] 'Well, there are similar points to bear in mind when throwing a javelin…'
explaining the structure of a lesson or unit, perhaps with reference to the learning objectives	'You are going to be planning and practising sequences of balances, rolls and travelling actions, with no more than five actions in a sequence. You are going to be working with a partner, so I would like to see lots of constructive comments on each other's work.'
giving meaning to a new concept or principle	'A basic strategy when defending in an invasion game is to reduce the space for the attacking team. In this lesson, we are going to be looking at ways to do this in hockey.'

- *Continuity*. A strong connecting thread should be maintained and evident throughout the lesson.
- *Simplicity*. Simple, intelligible and grammatical sentences should be used; too much information in sentences can lead to confusion and failure. The language used should be simple, and subject-specific vocabulary should always be defined and understood. Perrott also recommends that visual means can be used to help explain more complex relationships.
- *Explicitness*. One common cause of misunderstanding is the assumption that pupils understand more than they really do.

Examples can aid pupil understanding, provided that they are well chosen and presented. They can be particularly useful when introducing new material. Brown and Armstrong (1984) stress that examples should be clear, appropriate and concrete. They should also draw upon experiences that are familiar to pupils. Examples can be a valuable way of assessing understanding, as in the following instance: 'Do you all understand the different energy systems and how they relate to different types of physical activity? [Nodding agreement from pupils.] Good. Can anybody give me an example of an activity that relies upon the aerobic system?' Used in this way, examples can provide the teacher with an indication of understanding of the subject matter that goes beyond the pupils' ability to reproduce given explanations.

Task 5.2: Evaluating explanations

Ask a colleague or your mentor to observe you teach a lesson, and evaluate the extent to which you meet the criteria of good explanations (see Table 5.2 for an evaluation template for explanations). Discuss your strengths and weaknesses after the lesson, and agree targets for personal development.

Table 5.2   Evaluation template for explanations

Criteria	Always	Sometimes	Never	Example
explanation best way of giving information				
all pupils paying attention				
explanations concise, yet adequate				
logical presentation of information				
links with previous learning and experience				
simple, intelligible and grammatical sentences				
appropriate vocabulary used				
new terms defined and/or clarified				
use of concrete examples				
effective use of voice and gesture				
repetition of key concepts and phrases				
opportunity for pupil questions				
understanding assessed				
expectations made clear				

Demonstrations

The ability to provide clear, appropriate demonstrations is an essential skill in physical education lessons. Explanations are important, and can help pupils understand the concepts and skills being taught, but, when used alone, they can be limited in articulating visual information to pupils. Physical education lessons involve numerous presentations of visual information – patterns, shapes, directions, angles, speeds, movements, lack of movements and so on – and so the effective use of demonstrations alongside explanations becomes vital.

Demonstrations can serve a number of different purposes in physical education lessons:

- They provide a clear picture of the skill or task to be performed. Some learners, especially the young or inexperienced, can become confused by verbal explanations alone. Supplementing the explanation with a well-presented demonstration can aid understanding by combining a verbal with a visual reference (Christina and Corcos, 1988). In other words, people are more likely to understand and remember a task when they are both *told* and *shown* what to do.
- Demonstrations are particularly useful when the teacher needs to highlight a specific technical point. Many physical skills are made up of a host of smaller actions; a demonstration encapsulates these actions as a whole, and provides pupils with a model for their performance.
- They can also be a valuable motivational tool, celebrating the work of members of the class. This is acknowledged by Rowe (1997: 23), who writes: 'The kudos attached to demonstrating one's achievements to fellow classmates can be all too easily overlooked. A demonstration provides the PE teacher with a platform for the recognition of success/achievement.'
- Demonstration can be used to share ideas among the class. This is particularly useful where pupils or groups create their own movements, such as a dance routine or a gymnastics sequence. In dance, for example, giving each group the opportunity to show the others in the class their work in progress can provide a new source of ideas and motivation for the observers.
- Some concepts in physical education are easier to understand visually than verbally. Concepts like fluency in gymnastics, following through in throwing and body shape in swimming are easier to show than to explain.
- Sometimes a demonstration is just quicker for giving an idea of a task to pupils than offering a verbal explanation.
- Many activities in physical education use demonstration to show completed work. Dance, gymnastics, problem solving in outdoor activities, and games making are all examples of activities in which pupils work out their own solutions to challenges, and need an opportunity to show what they have done or achieved.

Presenting demonstrations

Demonstrations rely upon the sharing of visual information, so it is absolutely essential that all pupils can see. There are many different ways of arranging the group of observers so they are in a position to see the demonstration (and hear the teacher), such as semicircles, straight lines, and two rows, one behind the other. Older pupils can usually arrange themselves with a combination of sitters and standers around the demonstrator, but younger children will often need to be organized into an appropriate formation by the teacher. Whatever the format, it is useful to check that all can see clearly before proceeding. It is also important that pupils are not looking directly at the sun, nor at other distractions that could take their attention away from the demonstration.

It is also worth considering whether the observers can see all of the important aspects of the skill from one angle. Many tasks are best presented from more than one angle, and offering pupils a variety of viewpoints allows them to build up a fuller image of the skill. For example, the demonstrator can perform the forehand badminton stroke both facing and looking away from the class. The different angles reveal quite different features of the stroke and footwork. Other skills are better performed from one side and then the other. Another, often overlooked, factor is that of handed-ness. Every class is likely to be made up of both left- and right-handed players. If possible, the teacher should ensure than the skill is demonstrated for both groups.

When offering demonstrations to a class, the teacher needs to ensure that the pupils are attending to the relevant features of the performance. An effective way of ensuring this focused attention is through the use of learning cues, or words or phrases that highlight the key features of a skill or task. Rink (1993) suggests that good cues are: accurate; critical to the task being presented; few in number; and appropriate to the pupils' age and stage of learning. It can be a challenge for inexperienced teachers to choose relevant cues for all the activities taught in physical education lessons. However, there is little doubt that the selection of cues can make a great difference to pupil understanding and achievement. Planning is the key, and it is important that time is taken in the preparation of lessons to select the most appropriate learning cues for the tasks being taught. This may involve reference to textbooks, or discussions with more experienced colleagues.

Learning cues can take many forms. Some may simply be concise descriptions of the key features of the skill, such as 'Feet parallel', 'Eye on the ball', 'Follow through' and so on. But teachers can also be more adventurous with their language. Action words that accurately capture a feature of the skill can stick in pupils' minds, especially if accompanied by emphasis in tone; for example, runners might be told to *explode* off the mark, basketball shooters might *snap* their wrists and swimmers might *glide* through the water. Another approach is to engage pupils' imaginations through the use of metaphor and analogy. A well-chosen metaphor can help pupils remember concepts far better than bland instructions, and can also offer an insight into the quality of the movement to be carried out. For example, a teacher encouraging pupils to stretch as high as they can when serving in tennis might suggest that they imagine they are reaching up to clean cobwebs from the ceiling or waft away clouds; pupil gymnasts trying to improve their posture or control can imagine that they are being pulled upwards by a thread joining the top of their heads to the ceiling; the different wrist actions of off-breaks and leg-breaks in cricket can be compared to turning a doorknob one way or another. Dance lessons, of course, are frequently replete with wonderful metaphors and imaginative allusions.

Task 5.3

Select six skills or tasks that you will be teaching in the coming weeks. For each one, identify three or four (no more) learning cues. Discuss your list with your mentor or another experienced teacher, and ask him or her to assess the cues and the extent to which they are:

- accurate;
- critical to the task being presented;
- concise;
- appropriate to the pupils' ages and stages of learning.

Demonstrations by their nature should offer an accurate portrayal of the skill to be learnt, since pupils will generally try to reproduce what they see. If a demonstration contains errors, then the pupils' reproductions will also probably contain errors. Even if the teacher offers an accurate verbal explanation of a skill, but offers an inaccurate demonstration, most pupils will attend to the visual information and reflect the inaccuracy (Rink, 1993).

The notion of accuracy in demonstrations goes beyond the simple performance of the mechanics of the skill. Demonstrations should reflect, as nearly as possible, the context in which the observers will be performing the skill. So, it is unwise to offer just an element of the task, or perform the skill with a different speed or rhythm from the one it should have. If the teacher needs to emphasize a specific aspect of the task, it is worth ensuring that the pupils return to their practice with a clear understanding of the skill they will be required to practise, as well as the detail, firmly in their minds. The simplest way to do this is to 'sandwich' the detail between the whole skill performance, so that the observers understand the part within the context of the whole, as follows:

1. performance of whole skill/task;
2. break-up of skill/task, and demonstration of detail;
3. performance of whole skill/task.

Summarizing research on movement skill learning, Mawer (1995) writes that the image of the movement provided by a demonstration is initially stored in the observer's short-term memory, and the retention of this image is likely to be quite limited by time. If the skill is to be remembered for later recall, the learner needs to be given the opportunity to practise it soon after observing. This can be facilitated by organizing groups and practice areas before the demonstration, and by making expectations for practice clear.

Who should demonstrate?

Demonstrations should offer pupils a clear, accurate model of the skill or task to be performed. Therefore the selection of the demonstrator is of some significance. Perhaps the obvious person to show skills is the teacher, and this does have certain benefits, not the least of which is that the teacher knows (or should know) the key features of the skill to stress. However, a teacher who is demonstrating is not in an ideal position to monitor the class. Too heavy an emphasis on teacher demonstrations also robs the pupils of the opportunity of demonstrating themselves. One time when it is most appropriate for the teacher to demonstrate is when highlighting common errors: 'A number of you are making the same mistake. Now, I'll try to show you what you've been doing. I want you to watch me perform this stroke, and tell me what I am doing wrong.'

If pupils are used to demonstrate, it is important that this does not involve only a select few. More able pupils can provide a useful guide for certain complex skills. However, if these are the only or main pupils used, the rest of the class may come to feel rejected or of less value. Depending upon the skill being shown, even very poor performers can successfully contribute, especially if they are demonstrating a feature of the skill:

> Now, I would like you all to look at the way that Andrew, Sara and Michelle are all trying to move to space after passing the ball. They are not just standing there, waiting for the ball to come back to them. No, they are making it as easy as they can for their partner to pass the ball safely. I would like you all to try to move like that.

Interestingly, research suggests that imperfect demonstrations can be as effective as accurately performed ones, so long as the pupils have a clear understanding of the intention of the skill (Rink, 1999). Therefore, well-presented explanations and questions should supplement the visual input. Others have argued that watching someone who is not an expert, and who is going through the process of learning and receiving feedback, may actually contribute to the observer's learning (Pollock and Lee, 1992).

The advent of information and communication technology (ICT) in physical education lessons opens up new opportunities, and some of these relate to demonstrations. CD ROMs and video films can add greater flexibility to demonstrating by allowing pupils to play and replay, freeze-frame and rewind the action. Some technologies let pupils observe a skill from different angles, or zoom into a particular detail. A note of caution is required, though. Commercially produced films and disks are likely to be rather general and to contain too much information. It is always good practice for the teacher to use any resources selectively, and to pick those parts that meet the requirements for the lesson. Information and communication technology is supposed to support good teaching, not replace it (see Chapter 9, where the effective use of ICT is discussed in greater detail).

When to demonstrate?

A final decision to be made on the presentation of demonstrations is that of timing. When, during the lesson, should they be used? There are three different times to use demonstrations: before the pupils perform the skill; distributed throughout the practice session; and as a conclusion to the practice (Christina and Corcos, 1988).

Demonstrations before pupils perform the skill are usually intended to present a model of the skill for pupils to reproduce. Even skills that have been practised in previous lessons benefit from an initial presentation at the start of the lesson, if only to refresh pupils' memories of the learning cues. At this stage, a number of repetitions of the demonstration will be necessary, as will presenting the skill from different angles.

Once the session is under way, it may be worth while to break up the period with another demonstration, to help the learners focus again upon the key features of the skills. This can be combined with highlighting a particularly good example of the skill that the teacher has witnessed, which adds a motivational element to the demonstration. Younger children may need a repetition of the full demonstration, whilst older pupils may only require an abbreviated presentation, or a refinement of the original demonstration (Christina and Corcos, 1988). Another use for mid-lesson demonstrations is to address common errors that have arisen.

Demonstrations during the conclusion phase of the lesson are often used to celebrate pupils' work and achievement. For example, this may be an opportunity for groups to perform their dance routines or gymnastics sequences in front of their peers. A concluding demonstration can also act as a reinforcer of the learning cues and key points, in preparation for future lessons.

Criteria for effective demonstrations are suggested in Task 5.4 below.

Task 5.4

As an alternative to being observed by a colleague, try to video-record yourself teaching and evaluate your performance, paying particular attention to the quality of your demonstrations. Or, ask your mentor or a colleague to operate the video-recorder, and discuss the lesson together. Possible criteria for good demonstrations are listed below:

- All pupils are in a position to see the demonstration.
- All pupils are paying attention.
- No pupil is facing the sun or other avoidable distractions.
- Skill, or key feature of the skill, is accurately performed.
- The context for the skill or task is explained.
- The whole skill or task is shown as part of each demonstration.
- The skill or task is shown from a variety of angles.
- Appropriate learning cues are selected.
- Questioning is used to check understanding of learning cues.
- Pupils are given the chance to seek clarification.
- Pupils of all abilities are used for demonstrating.
- Expectations for practice are explained to the class.
- Pupils move to practise the skill quickly after the demonstration.

Questioning

Questioning is one of the most frequently employed teaching strategies (Wragg, 1993). Questions can be asked of individual pupils, groups or whole classes, and for a variety of reasons, including to arouse curiosity, focus attention, identify problems, communicate expectations, encourage reflection and assess. It is important to be clear about the reasons for asking a question, as this can ensure that it is phrased appropriately and achieves the result desired.

There are numerous ways of categorizing the types of questions teachers ask pupils. The simplest division is into *convergent* and *divergent* questions. Convergent (or closed) questions lead to a specific, correct answer ('What is the offside rule?'), whilst divergent (or open) questions provide the opportunity for a variety of possible answers ('How can we draw the dance to a close?'). There is some evidence to suggest that divergent questions are more suitable for encouraging higher-order thinking skills, but there is also an important place for factual, lower-order questions, too (Good and Brophy, 1991). In fact, teachers should use many different types of questions during lessons, depending upon what they are trying to achieve. Mawer (1995) suggests that it is the sequencing or combining of questions with particular objectives in mind that matters most. So convergent questions might be used initially to remind pupils of certain key facts, and then divergent questions used to help pupils apply their knowledge to a particular problem.

Some purposes for questions in physical education lessons are outlined in the box below.

Using questions for specific purposes

Questions that focus attention

Questions can be used that require pupils to pay attention to a specific feature of an action or a performance. These can solicit either affirmations that the pupils understand or notice the feature, a specific answer or a range of answers:

- 'Can you see how Jane is keeping her head forwards and over the ball when she plays the forward defensive stroke?'
- 'What is the main difference between the good and poor ways of holding a balance that I've just shown you?'
- 'Can you suggest three important points to remember when performing the front crawl?'

Questions that lead pupils to be mindful

It is very easy for any of us to adopt a mindless, unthinking way of operating, and this can result in poor-quality performance, missed learning and even accidents (Langer, 1989). Questions can therefore be used to make pupils think about what they are doing, or to reflect upon their actions:

- 'Why did you perform the sequence in that way, rather than the way you planned before?'
- 'Why is it important to take your watches and jewellery off before the lesson?'

Questions that assess knowledge and understanding

Questioning is a simple and effective way of informally assessing pupil understanding of a topic. It might involve a revision of something covered previously, a check of basic subject knowledge or a test of understanding for a new concept:

- 'What key points do you remember from last week's lesson?'
- 'What is the technical term for that?'
- 'When might you see this tactic being used in a game?'

Questions that invite enquiry

As well as consolidating knowledge, the use of questions should challenge pupils to think more deeply about principles and issues underpinning physical education. This might involve challenging pupils to think more diversely, to posit solutions to meaningful problems or to discuss questions of values:

- 'How many different ways can you think of for getting the ball over the net?'
- 'Team A is winning the ball too easily, isn't it? What can we do to make the game more balanced?'
- 'What's wrong with cheating?'

Questions that develop self- and peer-assessment skills

Pupils can play active roles in their own skill development, and carefully selected questions can help them identify relevant cues:

- 'Why do you think that was a good sequence?'
- 'How did John generate such force in his throw?'
- 'How could you improve on your performance next time?'

The importance of questioning should not be undervalued in its contribution to pupil learning. Indeed, in a review of good practice in primary schools, OFSTED (1994) found that questioning was the single most important factor in pupils' achievement of high standards, where questions were used to assess knowledge and understanding, and challenge thinking.

Planning is vital in effective questioning, and inexperienced teachers are advised to include relevant questions in their lesson plans. Different stages of the lesson will necessitate different types of questions, and these should be thoroughly prepared in advance if they are to be used to maximum effect. Table 5.3 offers a model of questioning during the lesson (loosely based on Cohen, Manion and Morrison, 1996).

There are a number of principles that support effective questioning. The most obvious, and important, is clarity. Questions should be stated clearly and concisely. Rushing or trying to include too many concepts is likely only to confuse pupils. Some physical education areas have poor acoustics, and it will be necessary to take some care to ensure that all pupils can hear the question. It is also important to make sure that they can all hear the answer, too, and it may be necessary for the teacher to repeat an answer to the class. Added benefits of repeating answers are that the teacher can emphasize parts of the answer, rephrase for clarity if necessary or add a point:

Teacher: What should we remember as we dribble around the area?
Pupil: Look where we're going.
Teacher: Why is looking important?
Pupil: So you can see where everyone is.
Teacher: Yes, that's right. Look. [Pause.] We need to be able to look where we are going so that we can see people to pass to or to shoot for goal. We also need to look so that we don't crash into other people!

If no one is able to answer a question, it may be necessary to rephrase it, or break it up into smaller, more manageable sub-questions.

Table 5.3 Relating question type to stage of lesson

Stage	*Types of Questioning*
Introduction	– to establish contact with class – to focus attention – as part of set induction – to assess knowledge and understanding of lesson theme – to recap previous lessons – to gain interest and curiosity
Main Part	– to maintain interest and attention – to assess understanding – to clarify – to address difficulties and misunderstandings – to stimulate self-assessment and reflection – to reinforce
Conclusion	– to recap on main points of the lesson – to assess extension and improvement – to prepare for next lesson – to allow expressions of feelings and views

Once a question has been asked, sufficient time should be allowed for the pupil to think and answer. This is particularly the case in problem-solving situations, or when a pupil has been asked to reflect upon an issue. Inexperienced teachers can become impatient or nervous during the silence whilst a pupil thinks, and either hurry an answer or move on to someone else. Ideally, the teacher should welcome more than one answer to a question before responding, as this encourages a sense of co-operation among members of the class and a realization that most answers are tentative.

A common complaint is that some teachers only seem to ask a relatively small proportion of the class questions. Some children may be keener to answer than others, and they can come to dominate discussions. Others stay silent, and are easily overlooked. In fact, some children can become highly proficient at becoming 'invisible' in the lesson (Pye, 1988). Most questioning and interaction during lessons seem to happen between the teacher and pupils positioned in a V-shaped area in front of the teacher. Those at the periphery are out of the action, and so it is to these areas that unwilling or confused pupils emigrate (Adams and Biddle, 1970). A simple, effective strategy to overcome this problem is for the teacher mentally to divide the class into zones, and to address a question to a pupil in each zone.

A related problem is when pupils are allowed to shout out answers to questions. Whilst enthusiasm should be encouraged, a free-for-all will only result in a loss of control and quieter pupils being overlooked. A simple routine should be established from the beginning, and consistently enforced, of putting hands up to answer questions.

Task 5.5

Some of the most common errors in questioning are listed below:

- too many convergent questions;
- lack of clarity;
- inappropriate vocabulary;
- allowing mass calling out of answers;
- repeatedly focusing upon the same pupils;
- not addressing the full range of abilities in the class;
- not allowing time for pupils to think and answer;
- illogical sequence of questions;
- ignoring answers;
- intolerant responses to incorrect answers;
- ejecting valid but unexpected answers.

Reflect upon your own performance, and consider the extent to which you are guilty of any of them.

> Rephrase the list positively, and ask a colleague or your mentor to observe and evaluate your teaching, focusing upon your positive criteria.

A final point needs to be considered in relation to questioning: it need not be a one-way relationship. A teacher–pupil relationship in which pupils feel able to ask sensible, relevant questions of the teacher is a positive one. Of course, lessons can be disturbed by too-frequent questioning of the teacher, and it is important to keep a sense of balance. Cohen, Manion and Morrison (1996) suggest inviting questions from the class at appropriate points in the lesson, such as after the introductory phase, which can help the inexperienced teacher maintain a sense of control of the lesson. Whatever way the teacher decides to accept questions, it is vital not to bluff pupils' questions. If you don't know the answer to a question, admit it. It is usually easy to spot when someone is hiding their ignorance, and this undermines a teacher's credibility much more than an honest admission of uncertainty, and a promise to try to find out the answer for the next lesson.

Interventions

Some people equate teaching with the initial presentation of activities to pupils, and overlook the equally important work of teachers as the lesson develops. Rink (1993: 146) notes that 'few beginning teachers give much thought to what happens after they ask learners to engage in a movement task or learning experience. This is an uncomfortable period in the instructional process for beginning teachers because, actually, what they do as teachers depends greatly on what the students do in relation to what the teachers asked them to do.' Providing guidance and feedback to pupils as they perform the tasks of a lesson is one of the most valuable contributions teachers can make to their pupils' learning.

Most physical education lessons involve one teacher and many more pupils, so the time available for guidance is strictly limited, and this time should be used wisely. The value of an intervention can be judged by the extent to which it contributes to the support and assistance of pupils' learning. The number and length of teacher interventions are less important than the quality of the interaction between teacher and pupil, and effective teachers develop sound judgements regarding the usefulness of intervening and how it compares with alternative courses of action. There are times when the teacher simply gets in the way of learning, by intervening when there is no need or by offering an inappropriate intervention.

Probably the most common form of intervention in physical education lessons is feedback, where the teacher gives information to pupils about their performance.

Feedback has been frequently cited as a feature of effective teaching strategies, and in their classic study, Fitts and Posner (1967: 183) have described its main functions: 'It can provide knowledge, motivation and reinforcement. It can also serve as a reward, providing extremely strong motivation to continue a task, since it relates to the distance between a present state and a goal. Since feedback operates as a strong source of motivation it may be an important or even necessary condition of learning.' However, more recent research in physical education lessons suggests that the virtues of feedback, in itself, might not be so clear cut (Rink, 1999).

There are a number of variables that influence the effect of feedback, including:

- learners' knowledge;
- the teacher's knowledge;
- the target of feedback;
- the form of feedback.

Learners' knowledge

Feedback from a teacher or coach is sometimes referred to as augmented feedback, to distinguish it from learners' own intrinsic feedback, provided through their own senses. Research suggests that there are certain situations where learners do not need a great deal of feedback from the teacher, and it may create a dependency on the part of learners, which is ultimately harmful to learning (Rink, 1999). Specifically, feedback may be unnecessary when learners have a clear idea of the skill they are trying to perform, and when they can rely upon their own intrinsic feedback. It can also be unnecessary in the early stages of learning, when pupils are familiarizing themselves with the language and basic movements of an activity. In most cases in physical education lessons, however, pupils are not in a position to do without feedback, so teacher guidance should make a valuable contribution to learning and improvement.

The teacher's knowledge

The above discussion is based on the assumption that teachers have sufficient and relevant knowledge to contribute to pupil understanding. This is not always the case, and insufficient knowledge on the part of the teacher can become a serious obstacle to pupil learning, especially when that teacher provides incorrect guidance. Research (reported in Mawer, 1995) suggests that more knowledgeable teachers provide more specific skill-related feedback for the correction of errors than those less knowledgeable. Teachers can considerably enhance their subject knowledge through continuing professional development. In the meantime, however, the most sensible precaution is thorough preparation and planning of lessons.

The target of the feedback

At different times during a lesson, a teacher may offer feedback to an individual, a group and the whole class. As has already been acknowledged, the time for intervention is strictly limited during physical education lessons, and one-on-one coaching is rarely an option, so alternative approaches are necessary. If an error is common to many pupils in a class, the teacher might work with those pupils as a group, or direct comments to an individual so that the whole class can hear (although Rink, 1993, warns against this sort of strategy with secondary pupils, for whom singling out for public feedback may have strong social consequences).

The form of the feedback

Some types of feedback may be more effective than others. Research (see Mawer, 1995) suggests that effective feedback is usually:

- congruent;
- specific;
- supportive.

Congruent feedback gives information on performance that is directly related to the learning points introduced by the teacher. Pupils should focus upon a relatively small number of cues when performing tasks set by the teacher, and effective feedback reinforces those cues. The alternative is what Rink (1993: 154) calls the 'shotgun approach', where the teacher asks pupils to focus upon a task, and then gives feedback on everything he or she knows or observes that is related to the skill. There may be occasions when the teacher offers guidance to pupils that goes beyond the original learning points, especially when pupils progress faster than expected and the teacher tries to extend achievement. However, this is more focused and deliberate than the random shotgun approach, and still relates to the planned aims of the unit of work:

> That is very good. In all of those catches you got behind the ball, kept your eyes on it until it was in your hands and cushioned the catch. Now I would like you to work as a group, and one at a time call for the ball before going to catch it. Call early, and be really loud and clear with your call.

There is considerable evidence to show that feedback that is *specific* makes a greater contribution to pupil learning than vague, general information (Mawer, 1995). Guidance that is specifically related to the learning cues of the task is much more likely to result in learning and appropriate responses. It also helps learners focus upon the details of the task at hand. More general feedback – 'Good', 'OK' or 'Not like that' – can be motivating for learners, but it is of little help in developing their skills. Two possible exceptions that make the rule are younger children and beginners. In these cases, it is often more useful for the teacher to offer supportive general comments, and allow the learners to explore different ways of carrying out the task, before progressing to more specific information on performance.

Positive feedback is generally preferable to negative comments. However, this is not to suggest that teachers should never tell pupils that they are wrong, as is sometimes assumed. Positive feedback focuses upon the positive features of a performance, and can be useful in highlighting achievements and future targets, such as: 'Well done, Clare. You are really starting to get your head over the ball.' Negative feedback may have a role, too, especially if pupils are repeatedly performing an action incorrectly or where there is a safety issue, for example: 'You are still not timing the handover of the baton as well as you need to do' or 'I don't want to see you bouncing when they stretch, because...' Since the labels 'positive' and 'negative' feedback have certain connotations, Mawer (1995) argues that it may be preferable to use the term '*supportive* feedback' for feedback that might have a combination of positive, negative and corrective elements.

Feedback can also be either evaluative or corrective (Rink, 1993). Evaluative feedback occurs when the teacher makes some sort of judgement about the past performance of a task. Corrective feedback offers guidance to the learner about ways of improving future performances. Teachers often use both forms together, as in: 'That was much better; now try to work on the synchronization with your partner.'

Table 5.4 provides a summary of the different forms of feedback.

Summary

The different skills and strategies at teachers' disposal constitute part of their professional toolkit, and, as with any tool, effectiveness depends upon appropriate use. There is a considerable amount of evidence that suggests that effective teachers are able to draw upon a wide range of teaching strategies and apply them in relevant contexts. Sadly, there is also evidence that physical educators, as professionals, often draw upon a narrow range of skills, and thus restrict pupils' opportunities to learn (Macfadyen, 2000a). This chapter has offered guidance on a range of

Table 5.4 Forms of feedback in physical education lessons (adapted from Rink, 1993)

Form	Evaluative	Corrective
Congruent*	'You had a long, thin shape as you glided.'	'Try to make your body as long and thin as you can.'
Incongruent*	'Your breathing isn't controlled.'	'Try to breathe in a controlled way and cup the water in your hands as you move into the stroke.'
Specific	'Your last balance had really good extension and control.'	'Try to point your toes a little more.'
General	'Excellent!'	'Don't do that.'
Positive	'Carrie orientated her map straight away.'	'Remember to orientate your map.'
Negative	'That is not good enough.'	'Don't slow down until you have crossed the line.'

* This assumes that the learning point is for the pupil to hold a long, thin body shape during the glide (in a swimming lesson).

teaching skills, and suggested ways in which those skills can support pupil learning.

Key points to remember include:

- Verbal information, such as instructions, explanations and feedback, can support skill learning and understanding, and should be provided in a concise, focused and meaningful form.
- Questioning provides a valuable, flexible tool for the teacher. Different types of questions relate to different types of training situations.
- Demonstrations should be accurate, critical to the task being presented, concise and appropriate to the pupils' ages and stages of learning.

Further reading

Macfadyen, T M (2000) The effective use of teaching styles, in *Teaching Physical Education 5–11*, ed R P Bailey and T M Macfadyen, Continuum, London

Mawer, M (1995) *The Effective Teaching of Physical Education*, Chapters 8, 9 and 10, Longman, London

Rink, J E (1999) Instruction from a learning perspective, in *Learning and Teaching in Physical Education*, ed C Hardy and M Mawer, Falmer Press, London

6 Managing behaviour

Introduction

This chapter addresses the challenging issue of dealing with pupil misbehaviour. It should not be considered as isolated in any way from earlier discussions of planning, organization and teaching. These different features are inextricably linked: learning and teaching are premised on appropriate pupil behaviour; good behaviour is most likely to arise in the context of effective teaching strategies. Problems with discipline and control are matters of particular concern for trainee and inexperienced teachers, and so it is necessary for them to be familiar with a range of approaches for dealing with both minor and more serious difficulties.

Objectives

By the end of this chapter you should:

- understand the importance of a positive approach to class management and control;
- be aware of the types of misbehaviour likely to occur during physical education lessons;
- understand possible causes of such misbehaviour;
- be familiar with strategies for dealing with both minor and major incidents of misbehaviour.

Positive class management and control

'Discipline is what you do when, in spite of your best efforts, students do not co-operate and choose to behave in appropriate ways' (Rink, 1993: 140).

Maintaining discipline is probably the greatest cause for concern among trainee and newly qualified teachers. Mawer (1995) reports that 60 per cent of heads of department questioned rated control and discipline as being the major concerns and difficulties experienced by those new to teaching physical education. This group also saw the establishment of control and discipline as essential foundations for trainees. In the words of one head of department: 'Control and discipline are crucial. It should underpin everything you do. With me discipline and control come first. Once established you can get on with teaching and enjoyment, without discipline and control there can be only chaos and potential danger' (Mawer, 1995: 124).

In considering discipline and control strategies, it is important to recognize that they cannot be viewed in isolation from the skills of planning, class management and teaching discussed in earlier chapters of this book. Whilst there are tips and skills that can be learnt and applied to improve the teacher's control, they should be understood within the context of effective teaching in general. As Cohen, Manion and Morrison (1996) emphasize, discipline is a 'built-in' element of teaching, not a 'bolt-on' extra. It affects every aspect of school life, pupil achievement and child welfare.

The discipline strategies employed by physical educators of the past have not always reflected the positive approach advocated in this book and promoted throughout the modern profession. Indeed, the bullying 'sportsmaster' is now a staple comedy stereotype. Think of the classic portrayal of the physical education teacher in the film, *Kes*, or more recently in the television series, *The Grimleys*: shouting, threatening, teasing, punishing and making lessons unbearable for all pupils, especially the less able. Such behaviour is totally unsatisfactory and should be a thing of the past. One consequence of such approaches seems to be that some people come to look back at their physical education experiences with negative feelings, and come to be reluctant to participate in physical activities after leaving school, with the associated risks to health and fitness of such a withdrawal (Lambirth and Bailey, 2000).

Today, teachers are aware of the intrinsic link between generally effective teaching and good control and management strategies. Teachers who can produce well-planned and well-presented lessons are also those who maintain the most order and engender a positive working environment (Rink, 1993). Relationships between pupils and teachers play a great role in the establishment and maintenance of a positive working environment, as is suggested by Cooper and MacIntyre's (1996) summary of research in this area. Research shows that effective teachers relate to their pupils in ways that stress their positive regard for pupils, and they strive to take careful account of individual differences among their pupils, even when teaching large groups. These teachers also encourage active participation in lessons, use praise and create conditions that help to encourage pupils to perform well.

It is worth stressing that nearly all pupils want to achieve and co-operate in physical education lessons nearly all of the time. Serious acts of misbehaviour are rare and, whilst they cannot be overlooked, their rarity echoes the fact that most pupils are very keen to learn and be taught. When asked for their views on what makes a good teacher, pupils' answers resemble very closely those that might be offered by teachers. For example, one study of Scottish 12-year-olds' views of the characteristics of good teachers (cited in Cohen, Manion and Morrison, 1996) found that pupils regarded favourably teachers who kept order, were strict and punished pupils; who actually taught them and kept them busy with work; who gave explanations, were helpful and could be understood; who were interesting, unusual and different; who were fair, consistent and had no favourites; and who were friendly, kind, talked and joked. It is likely that teachers would offer general agreement to a model of teacher competence based on their criteria (see Wragg and Wood, 1984b).

Some of the principles of positive class management strategies outlined in earlier chapters of this book include the following:

- Maintain a positive, purposeful working environment.
- Establish effective class management and organization systems.
- Implement a workable, shared set of rules and routines.
- Plan and deliver challenging and rewarding activities.
- Make sure pupils understand the reasons why they are doing the activities.
- Encourage high standards and value pupils' effort and performance.
- Plan for and teach in recognition of individual needs and differences.
- Be clear in articulating and sharing expectations with pupils.
- Be firm and fair.
- Develop positive, supportive relationships with pupils.
- Organize time and space to facilitate maximum learning and participation.

One must acknowledge that there are times when the positive working environment facilitated by such strategies breaks down, and the teacher needs to draw upon a wider range of skills to maintain control and discipline. Some teachers new to the profession express feelings of guilt when disciplining pupils, and can seem permissive, ineffectual and 'soft'. As was found above, this is not the approach that is valued by most pupils. They want to work and learn, and they recognize that a firm teacher, with control over the class and a range of discipline strategies at his or her disposal, is the person most likely to provide the necessary environment. Robertson's (1989: x) wise words are very apposite in this respect: 'Children are not the victims of classroom control, they are the beneficiaries.'

Types of misbehaviour

Appropriate planning, well-established rules and routines, and effective management strategies make a great contribution to class control. However, acts of misconduct may arise during even the best-planned and delivered lessons.

Misbehaviour can take many forms, from annoyances like noise to overt aggression or violence. The influential Elton Report on *Discipline in Schools* (DES/ WO, 1989) found that the most troublesome behaviour for teachers was usually not serious misconduct, but rather irritating minor disturbances and breaches of discipline, such as talking out of turn, interfering with the work of others and work avoidance. It is these relatively insignificant acts that occur most frequently and can drain teachers' energy and enthusiasm.

It is important to distinguish between different classes of misbehaviour, since inappropriate responses can lead to a worsening of a situation: a teacher who over-reacts to silly nuisances is as likely to have difficulties as one who under-reacts to major problems. However, it is wise to recognize that minor acts can easily escalate into more serious types, if not dealt with efficiently.

Task 6.1

Compile a list of the types of misbehaviour that might occur during physical education lessons. This might be based upon your own experiences as a pupil or as a teacher, or from observations of others' lessons. Discuss your list with your mentor or other experienced colleagues, and extend the list if necessary.

Once you have developed a fairly comprehensive list of types of misbehaviour, try to distinguish between those acts that you believe to be relatively minor and those that are more serious. What criteria did you use to help you separate the two groups? What are the implications of these types of misbehaviour in terms of pupils' learning, your teaching, safety?

Two useful studies offer support for the contention made earlier that serious acts of misconduct are very rare. Wragg's (1993) observational study of primary classrooms found that only 2 per cent of the deviant behaviour observed fell outside of their criteria for 'mild'. However, he also found that these mild acts of misbehaviour occurred frequently: in about half of the lesson segments observed. Most of these cases involved pairs or groups of pupils, and often these groups were made up of boys working together. The most common kind of misbehaviour observed was noisy or illicit talking, followed by inappropriate movement and inappropriate use of materials.

Similar results were found in Hardy's study of 39 secondary physical education lessons (cited in Hardy, 1999). He found that the most frequently occurring types of misbehaviour during lessons were (in descending order):

- not paying attention during the teacher's instructions (eg talking to another pupil);
- not carrying out the teacher's instructions (eg not doing the task as directed);
- disrupting others (eg interfering with others' performance of skills);
- refusing to take part in the lesson (eg refusing to co-operate in a task);
- not carrying out the policy procedure (eg wearing inappropriate clothing or jewellery);
- wishing to be the centre of attention (eg pulling faces).

Causes of misbehaviour

It is difficult to identify precisely the causes of misbehaviour in physical education lessons. Pupils are, after all, individuals, and as such they approach school with their own unique perspectives, needs and problems. Or, as a newly qualified teacher (quoted by Mawer, 1995: 126) put it: 'There are so many things that can affect the outcome of a lesson. You have 20–30 people bringing their own personal baggage with them to a lesson. There is no doubt that they will have varied expectations and intentions.'

Some pupils may be predisposed to misbehave during physical education lessons before they even turn up for the lesson. Drawing on a number of sources, Cohen, Manion and Morrison (1996) identify some of the main patterns of disruptive behaviour arising from social or emotional causes. They include:

- antipathy;
- social dominance;
- social isolation;
- inconsequential behaviour;
- conflicting rules;
- anxiety;
- leadership styles.

Teachers should try to understand the reasons for misbehaviour and address their responses accordingly. Therefore, it is worth spending a little time looking at this list, from a physical education perspective.

Antipathy

Feelings of antipathy are associated with pupils who have come to the conclusion that school or parts of it have no relevance for them. The problem of antipathy seems to be a relatively rare problem in physical education classes, which are, after all, among the most popular for pupils. However, research does show that many girls do acquire a progressive disillusionment with the subject as they move through secondary school. There are a number of likely reasons for this, including boys' dominance in certain activities and a perception that the National Curriculum is biased towards traditionally 'male' activities, combined with social pressure to conform to standards of femininity and a low priority given to female sporting achievement in society (Green and Scraton, 1998). Moreover, a physical education curriculum centred on competitive games, such as the current National Curriculum model, fails to match the leisure activities young women are most likely to take up on leaving school, such as aerobic dance. In this context, some girls dismiss physical education as 'unfeminine, irrelevant and childish' (Kay, 1995: 59). So, some young women can come to develop a sense of antipathy towards physical education, which may lead to misbehaviour or avoidance, evidenced by the fact that, whilst 11- and 12-year-old girls show no difference from boys of the same age in their likelihood to excuse themselves from lessons, by the time they reach 15 and 16 years, girls are twice as likely to miss physical education.

Task 6.2

Physical education should be relevant and meaningful for all pupils. Discuss the problem of antipathy with your mentor or head of department:

- Is there a perceived problem of girls' rejection of the subject? (Remember, there may be a problem, even if it is recognized by the staff.)
- Are there any other groups or individuals in school who show antipathy towards physical education lessons?
- What strategies have been put into place to address the threat of antipathy and avoidance of physical education?

Social dominance

Cohen, Manion and Morrison (1996: 303) quote Saunders, who views social dominance as an extension of the problem of antipathy:

Some physically and socially mature pupils seem to have a need for frequent reinforcement in the form of attention from their peers. This is often achieved at school by challenging the authority of the teacher. If the challenge is not met it can be taken up by other pupils and the lesson ruined, and as a result the assertion of the teacher's authority becomes more difficult in future lessons.

Machismo posturing is a common problem for teachers, and may be even more common within physical education lessons, where such behaviour may be exhibited by pupils and teachers alike. Flintoff (1998) identifies two strategies used by male trainee physical education teachers to assert their masculinity: overt demonstrations of physical prowess and competitiveness, and what she calls 'heterosexual displays'. Some older pupils may come to take this posturing as a challenge to which they should rise. However, even if such displays are accepted by socially dominant members of a class, it only serves to reinforce and legitimize reproductions of such behaviour directed towards less dominant members of the class.

Social isolation

Some pupils find themselves at the periphery of social groups and, in an attempt to win favour and acceptance from their peers, they can exhibit an extreme form of the group's behaviour. Therefore, if some pupils are misbehaving in a trivial way, an isolated pupil may cause a more serious transgression. Some pupils, however, may respond to being marginalized from their peers by overemphasizing their alienation, through acts of malice towards others in the group.

Inconsequential behaviour

Some pupils seem unable to anticipate the consequences of their actions, and others may find that problems with maintaining attention interfere with learning. Some people have suggested that there is an identifiable condition called 'attention deficit hyperactivity disorder' (ADHD), which relates to the important relationship between attending skills and the ability to learn. Pupils with ADHD may have significant problems with inattentiveness and impulsivity. Within the context of physical education, pupils with ADHD may seem not to listen, are easily distracted and have difficulties concentrating on tasks. This can present problems of safety, as well as of learning and understanding. Pupils can also appear restless and fidgety, and teachers often assume that misbehaviour is a wilful act on the part of the child.

Conflicting rules

Difficulties can arise when pupils are presented with sets of incompatible rules or expectations. For example, standards of behaviour at home may be different from those at school, or standards within one subject may clash with those in another. Most pupils are able to recognize that different rules apply in different contexts, and can adapt accordingly. Sometimes, however, it is necessary to discuss the matter with the pupils involved and seek a negotiated settlement (see Cohen, Manion and Morrison, 1996, for a possible approach).

Anxiety

Pupils who feel nervous, anxious or fearful are more likely to misbehave than their peers. Physical education, by its nature, provides unique opportunities for pupils to be adventurous, to test their limits and to excel. The danger, however, is that one pupil's challenge can easily become another's fear. Think about the range of activities within physical education in which pupils are expected to push themselves physically and mentally, and usually in a public forum, where their deficiencies are seen by all. A great deal of sensitivity is needed on the part of teachers to strike a balance, different for each pupil, between boredom and anxiety.

Leadership styles

Certain leadership or teaching styles can incite behaviour problems rather than solve them. Some teachers may come across to pupils as bullying and aggressive, and their teaching approach seems to have more to do with beating a class into submission than with learning and fulfilment. Others appear weak and over-permissive, reluctant to enforce rules and confront challenges. Pupils respond negatively to both. In the case of the bullying teacher, there is either an angry or a subversive response from the pupils. In the case of the weak teacher, pupils feel able to push the boundaries of acceptable behaviour further and further back, effectively making teaching and learning impossible. Pupils prefer a teacher who walks a middle ground between these extremes. Pupils are most likely to respond positively to a teacher who is:

- firm, but fair;
- relaxed, but in control;
- confident, but caring;

- businesslike, but humorous;
- in charge of the class, but aware of individual differences and needs.

It is also important to acknowledge that there may be 'pay-offs' for pupil misbehaviour. Robertson (1989) emphasizes that pupils can gain some benefits from misbehaving, and teachers may unwittingly be encouraging the very behaviours they wish to remove. Some of the motives for inappropriate behaviour include attention seeking, the avoidance of work, and excitement.

It is likely, however, that most acts of misbehaviour are connected to lesson content or management. In Fernandez-Balboa's (1991) study, for example, the main cause of pupil misconduct was 'boredom', followed by lack of interest in physical education, and then the personal characteristics of the pupil, such as hyperactivity. The principles of effective planning and teaching discussed elsewhere in this book should therefore be seen as fundamentally linked with the promotion of appropriate behaviour. It is also possible to identify those features of ineffective planning and teaching most likely to be associated with disturbances and misbehaviour.

Misbehaviour is most likely to arise if:

- the task is not of an appropriate level of challenge;
- instructions are not presented clearly;
- equipment is not readily available;
- the teacher arrives after the pupils have started to arrive;
- pupils feel that the teacher is unfair, or treats some pupils preferentially;
- pupils are bored with an activity;
- pupils are unable to perform the activity;
- pupils cannot see the point of the task;
- transitions between activities are not smooth and well organized;
- the teacher needlessly interrupts pupils during the task.

Managing 'proto'-misbehaviour

'Proto'-misbehaviour refers to those acts of misconduct that are relatively minor in themselves, but that might, if unchecked, progress to more serious discipline problems. Behaviours like talking out of turn, interfering with others and the avoidance of work can be irritating and tiresome, but are not, in themselves, serious disciplinary offences. There may be a case, therefore, for overlooking such minor acts, in case the teacher's actions cause more disturbance than the original problem. However, as Cohen, Manion and Morrison (1996) point out, this deliberate ignoring of minor indiscipline may be misconstrued by the pupils as either weakness or lack of awareness. Experience will better prepare the teacher to make reliable judgements about the relative merits of ignoring or addressing certain minor misbehaviours, but such experience is precisely what new teachers lack. So, it is wiser for trainee and newly qualified teachers to adopt a policy of 'zero tolerance', and show their control and awareness by dealing with all acts of misbehaviour as they arise, although this need not involve any disturbance to the rest of the class.

The effective use of non-verbal behaviour, movement around the physical education area, focused questioning and group reorganization can each cause minimum fuss, and can often remove the problem or its cause. By restricting the use of more overt, dramatic strategies for more serious crimes, their sheer rarity increases the likelihood that they will have the desired effect. Some strategies for dealing with proto-misbehaviour are outlined below.

Scanning

Scanning is a key skill for all teachers, and involves a conscious effort on the part of the teacher to look periodically around the area to ensure that all pupils are on task. The teacher's position needs to be one that offers a view of the whole space, although it is worth while not to become 'stuck' in one place, since this offers predictable hiding places for the mischievous. As pupils see that the teacher is scanning and moving around the area, they are more likely to remain on task and out of trouble. A teacher with this level of awareness is able to spot potential difficulties and disturbances, and deal with them quickly and effectively before they have time to grow into more serious problems.

Eye contact

Making and maintaining eye contact can be a subtle, effective way of showing misbehaving pupils that the teacher is aware of their behaviour, without disturbing other pupils in the class. Eye contact and the 'teacher's stare' are among the most frequently used tools of teachers, and are usually very effective in showing awareness and control. If necessary, the teacher might stop talking or stop what he or she is doing to underline the point. This can also be accompanied by authoritative body language, such as the folding of arms or a disapproving raise of the eyebrows. However, there is no value in engaging in staring contests with pupils. McManus (1994) suggests that averting eyes sideways (and not submissively downwards) if the stare is returned in an uncomfortable or defiant manner by a pupil can sometimes prevent the escalation of an unwanted act.

Proximity control

Rink (1993: 140) describes proximity control as when the teacher moves 'physically closer to the student to make known that they are aware that inappropriate behaviour is taking place'. This can be done without speaking to the pupil, or it can be combined with a simple question like 'How are you doing at this?' Again, there is minimal disturbance to the rest of the class, but the misbehaving pupil is brought back on task. It can also lead to a 'ripple effect', whereby other pupils are made aware of the teacher's attention.

Desists

Sometimes, the simplest and most efficient approach to inappropriate behaviour is to ask the offending pupils to stop, although it should be used sparingly for greatest effect. 'Desists work only if they are not overused. If a teacher has to continually remind the same student or if a class of students is behaving inappropriately, desists are *not working* and it is time to move on to other techniques that address the issues more seriously' (Rink, 1993: 140). It is preferable to keep the spoken comment between the teacher and the pupil, in order to avoid disturbing the rest of the class or running the risk of initiating a confrontation. When speaking, the teacher should maintain a firm, but pleasant, manner. Sarcasm and aggression are not appropriate. Sometimes, desists can effectively be rephrased as positive, so that the teacher tells the pupil what to do rather than what not to do.

Questioning

A well-focused question can remind misbehaving pupils of the task they are supposed to be carrying out, as well as remind them that the teacher is aware of their behaviour. If, as is likely, the questioned pupils are unable to answer the question, the teacher can follow up with some suggestions regarding better ways of working.

Relocation

It is sometimes the case that pupils are distracted through working in a particular space or with certain partners. For example, some young children can be easily distracted if they are working near a busy corridor or window. Likewise, some pupils are more likely to misbehave if they are close to others who encourage such misconduct. The simplest strategy is to move them to a new, less 'exciting' part of the hall.

Examples of the applications of these strategies are given in Table 6.1.

Reprimanding pupils

The strategies discussed above are useful because they offer minimal disturbance to the work of the class, whilst maintaining a positive working environment. However, there are times when such approaches don't have the desired effect of fully stopping misbehaviour, and further skills are required. Reprimanding misbehaving pupils is a valuable tool for the teacher, but should be used sparingly, since

Table 6.1 'Proto'-misbehaviour and control strategies

Scenario	Possible Strategy
During a problem-solving task in an outdoor and adventurous activities lesson, a group are off task and chatting.	*Questioning* 'What ideas have you come up with so far?'
Pupils are 'going through the motions' during a tennis skills practice, but are not working to their normal standard.	*Proximity control* The teacher moves near the group to a visible position and observes.
Whilst giving instructions to a class for a basketball lesson, a pupil is absent-mindedly bouncing a ball.	*Stop talking* The teacher pauses for a moment, until the pupil stops the action.
A pupil acts in an attention-seeking way during a dance practice.	*Eye contact* The teacher establishes and maintains eye contact with the pupil.
A pupil enters the gym in a noisy fashion.	*Desist* The teacher takes the pupil to one side and reminds him or her that one of the rules of the gym is that everybody enters quietly and sensibly.
Two pupils are not co-operating whilst planning their individual gymnastics floorwork sequences.	*Relocating* The teacher removes the pupils from the cause of the problem by giving each a new partner.

it threatens to undermine the positive working climate. Nagging teachers are not effective teachers.

McManus (1994: 199) offers a valuable reminder: 'It is easy to underestimate the need to make requirements explicit.' In other words, in reprimanding pupils the teacher should always seek to make clear to them the desired alternative behaviour. An example of this strategy is provided during a hockey lesson: 'John! You are swinging your stick too high, and there is a danger that you are going to hit someone. Now I want you to make sure that you keep it low. Can you remember the rule for stick height?' In this scenario, the teacher has stopped the hazardous action, highlighted the danger and directed the pupil towards a more appropriate action.

Loud, public rebukes can be counter-productive, unless used very infrequently. Their repeated use suggests lack of control and weakness. Mawer (1995) suggests that reprimands should be delivered firmly and directly, and that their impact should be enhanced by the use of eye contact and pause: 'reprimand – stare – pause for effect'. Threats should be used very sparingly, and not at all if the teacher has no intention of following through with them. Reprimands should be delivered immediately following the deed being rebuked, and should be controlled and brief. Brevity, in particular, is a virtue, since it ensures that there is as little disturbance as possible. Long-drawn-out diatribes are unlikely to have the desired effect, and usually have the opposite. Consider two examples. The first reprimand (reported in Wragg and Wood, 1984a) was delivered to a class of 13-year-olds:

> Are you eating? Well stop moving your jaws. Sit still. Some of you should be in straitjackets. If you don't work then you'll have to copy out of the book. You are going to conform to my standards, which are not in any way abnormal. In this life there are some people who want to work, there will be six million unemployed in the 1980s – none of you has convinced me that you are in any way employable. I'm in charge here. I can enforce it and will. It's as simple as that [bangs fist on the table]. Sooner or later someone will get physically hurt. Don't push me too far. We're all human, boys and girls alike. You are my family. It is my legal right to punish you. Don't forget that.

The second reprimand (observed by the author) was given to a class of six-year-olds:

> Just stop what you are doing and sit down, please. What in the world is going on with you today? You are being noisy and silly, and I am worried that someone is going to get hurt. Now, who can tell me what you are supposed to be doing? [Pupil raises hand, and answers]… Yes, so that is what I would like to see all of you doing.

Task 6.3

Reread the two reprimands above:

- What messages about the teachers' different levels of authority and control were put across?
- How do you imagine the pupils would have responded to the different rebukes?
- What effects would these two reprimands have upon the working climate?

In reprimanding a pupil, the teacher should make it clear that it is the behaviour, not the person, that the teacher is rejecting. Personal abuse has no place in physical education lessons, nor do comments designed to undermine pupils' self-esteem. It is not appropriate to compare pupils' behaviour: 'Why can't you behave more like Susan?' Likewise, the use of sarcasm or ridicule at the pupil's expense can lead to resentment, and possibly rejection of the subject itself.

Private reprimands are preferable to public ones, unless the aim is to share the point with the whole class. Mawer (1995) suggests giving the rebuke quietly and turning the pupil away from the rest of the group, to remove the possibility of playing up to the others. If the pupil responds emotionally, it may be better to delay the rebuke until the end of the lesson, and avoid a public argument.

Confrontations

Teachers rarely win confrontations with pupils. They indicate that the teacher has lost control of the situation and, whatever the short-term effect, there is a danger that the teacher's authority will have been undermined. Nevertheless, confrontations may still arise, and need to be dealt with effectively.

Pik (1981) proposes four principles that can assist teachers to deal with confrontational situations. First, the teacher needs to assess whether it is worth risking a confrontation over a particular incident. Does the act constitute a significantly serious misconduct that warrants intervention now, or would it be better dealt with at the end of the lesson? Second, give the pupil an 'out'. If the situation has escalated from a relatively minor incident, the pupil may be looking for a way out of the confrontation that saves face. Offering a compromise (or an apparent one) can provide this option. Third, the teacher needs to make sure that his or her behaviour, voice and body language do not appear aggressive and threatening, as this may provoke an aggressive response in reply, especially from older pupils.

Finally, if possible, attempt to re-establish normal relationships after the event. This need not involve a serious discussion of the quarrel. Robertson (1989) suggests that it can sometimes be useful to behave as if the incident had never happened, for example by talking to the pupils in a friendly way or asking a small favour of them, such as asking them to help set up equipment or demonstrate an action.

A 'time-out' can be a useful technique for handling continued disruptive behaviour, although Rink (1993) warns that it only works for young children and pupils who actually want to participate. It offers a time to reflect and consider the misconduct. The time-out area must be within the physical education area, so that the teacher can maintain surveillance at all times. If possible, it should be in a relatively quiet area, away from the action of the lesson.

Whole-class indiscipline

Misbehaviour involving most or all of a class is quite rare in physical education lessons, and is most likely to occur if individual or group problems are not dealt with effectively (Hardy, 1999). It is usually sensible to address the difficulty straight away, since it is unlikely that it will resolve itself. The whole-class reprimand can take the same form as that to an individual: address the problem behaviour and suggest an alternative. It can be useful to set some conditions of participation, such as a specific standard of behaviour. If the class fails to match that standard, the teacher should stop them again. If the problem continues, perhaps the best strategy is to take a break from the activity for a period of time. Assuming that most of the pupils wish to take part in the lesson, a minute sitting in silence can help them refocus on acceptable standards of behaviour. Some teachers call this the 'waiting game': they wait, without anger or frustration, until an acceptable standard of behaviour has been reached. If some pupils still misbehave, then the teacher may need to consider the use of punishment.

Punishment

Punishment is usually a last resort. Good control and discipline are premised upon appropriate planning, effective teaching strategies and established class management procedures. The need for punishment arises when these factors break down or are overridden. Good and Brophy (1991: 239) strike a note of caution: 'punishment can control misbehaviour, but by itself it will not teach desirable behaviour or even reduce the desire to misbehave. Thus, punishment is never a solution by itself; it can only be part of a solution.'

As has been discussed already, there is a variety of forms of misbehaviour, and most are effectively addressed with strategies other than punishment. The Elton Report (DES/WO, 1989) offered a list of approaches for dealing with misbehaviour, graded from least to most serious:

- reasoning with a pupil within the teaching area;
- reasoning with a pupil outside the teaching area;
- setting extra work;
- deliberately ignoring minor infractions;
- keeping pupils in after school;
- discussing with the whole class why things are going wrong;
- temporarily withdrawing a pupil from the class;
- referring a pupil to another teacher;
- removing privileges;
- sending a pupil to a senior figure in the school;
- involving parents;
- suspension from the school.

Good and Brophy (1991) stress that punishment is appropriate only for dealing with repeated misbehaviour, not a singular instance. It should also not be used when it is apparent that the pupil is trying to improve. Cohen, Manion and Morrison (1996) suggest some types of punishments that are best avoided:

- School work should not be used as a punishment. Pupils should not be punished for misbehaviour in one subject by being forced to do work from another. The most common form of this strategy in primary schools is where pupils are prevented from doing physical education, which is viewed as 'fun', and made to do maths or spelling, which is not.
- Avoid whole-class punishments, such as keeping all pupils in, when only a small number were involved in the misconduct.
- Forms of mental punishment, like personal criticism, ridicule and sarcasm, are inappropriate.
- Physical punishment is forbidden in British state schools.
- Only send a pupil to the head teacher as a last resort, or when confronted with a particularly serious case of misbehaviour. Such action weakens the teacher's personal authority. However, do not hesitate to seek advice privately from other members of staff.
- Avoid banishing a pupil from the gym or hall. If possible, keep the pupil in the physical education area.

Ultimately, punishment is a whole-school issue, and all schools have well-established policies for dealing with serious offences. There are also 'local' policies, within physical education departments. These set out normal sanctions and punishments available to teachers.

> ## Task 6.4
>
> Ask your mentor for a copy of the school (and, if available, physical education) policy documents for discipline and behaviour. Read these documents, and familiarize yourself with the accepted sanctions and punishments used in the school.
>
> All use of sanctions and punishments must be in accord with these documents, so discuss a range of scenarios and appropriate responses with your mentor.

Summary

This chapter has examined the principles of effective control and discipline. Although serious indiscipline is rare in physical education lessons, minor forms of misbehaviour can interfere with learning and the maintenance of a positive class environment. Key points from the chapter include:

- Prevention is more effective than cure. Positive class management and interpersonal relationships are the foundations of control and discipline.
- Control strategies are most likely to succeed when they accurately respond to situations. So, it is worth trying to understand the possible causes of specific problems.
- Criticize the behaviour, not the pupil.

Further reading

Cohen, L, Manion, L and Morrison, K (1996) *A Guide to Teaching Practice*, Chapter 14, Routledge, London

DES/WO (1989) *Discipline in Schools* (The Elton Report), HMSO, London

Hardy, C (1999) Student misbehaviours and teachers' responses in physical education lessons, in *Learning and Teaching in Physical Education*, ed C Hardy and M Mawer, Falmer Press, London

7

Special educational needs and differentiation

Introduction

This chapter addresses an issue of great importance and relevance for all teachers: special educational needs. It discusses the concepts of special educational needs and inclusive education, and interprets their meaning in terms of physical education provision. It goes on to suggest a range of strategies for identifying, planning and teaching for a wider range of needs in lessons. Underlying this chapter is an assumption that all pupils, whatever their ability or need, have an entitlement to a broad, balanced and dynamic physical education, and that this should ordinarily take place alongside their peers.

Objectives

By the end of this chapter you should:

- understand the key concepts underlying special educational needs in physical education;
- understand the conditions likely to lead to a special educational need in physical education;
- be aware of a range of differentiation strategies that can help the teacher to meet the needs of all pupils;
- know a simple assessment procedure for identifying and addressing special needs.

What are special needs in physical education?

'All teachers... are now teachers of children with special educational needs' (Jowsey, 1992: xv).

Current conceptions of special educational needs (SEN) owe a great deal to the Warnock Report (DES, 1978) and the subsequent Education Act of 1981, which argued against any simplistic views on special needs. Specifically, they rejected the sort of thinking that divided children into two groups: the handicapped and the non-handicapped, or those who go to special schools and those who do not. The Report emphasized that the complexities of individual needs are far more complex than such distinctions suggest, and offered as a replacement the concept of special educational needs. One of the most far-reaching outcomes of the Warnock Report and the 1981 Education Act was an estimation that at some time during their time at school, *one in five pupils* will require some sort of special provision. By current estimates, about two-thirds of pupils with statements of special educational needs attend mainstream schools (Black, 1999).

There are a number of ways of defining special educational needs. One approach is related to the special provision required to meet certain pupils' needs. For example, the *Code of Practice on the Identification and Assessment of Special Educational Needs* (DFE, 1994, para 2.1) defines a child as having a special educational need if he or she:

a) has a learning difficulty that calls for a special educational provision to be made;
b) has a significantly greater difficulty in learning than the majority of children of the same age;
c) has a disability that either prevents or hinders the child from making use of educational facilities of a kind provided for children of the same age in schools within the area of the LEA;
d) is under 5 and falls within the definition at (a) or (b) above or would do if special educational provision were not made for the child.

Another approach is to consider the types of needs pupils may have. The National Curriculum Council (NCC, 1992) classified these needs into four broad categories:

1. pupils with exceptionally severe learning difficulties;
2. pupils with other learning difficulties, including mild, moderate and specific learning difficulties and emotional and behavioural difficulties;
3. pupils with physical or sensory impairments;
4. exceptionally able pupils.

The inclusion of exceptionally able pupils in this list serves to reiterate the importance of avoiding a 'deficiency' or 'pathology' view of special educational needs that confines itself to pupils with learning difficulties or disabilities. It is also important to be cautious in generalizing about pupils' needs. For example, there is no reason to assume that a child with an emotional and behavioural difficulty (EBD) or specific learning difficulties (SPLD) necessarily has any lack of intelligence or physical competence. In other words, teachers should be careful not to give too much weight to labels, as this can easily lead to low expectations of pupils who depart from the 'norm'.

Types of needs

Physical education makes distinctive demands on pupils and carries unique curriculum content. A great deal of the literature on the subject of special needs assumes that children are being taught in classroom situations, that literacy and numeracy are the primary skills employed in these lessons and that, therefore, special needs will often be with regard to learning in this rather restricted sense. However, much of the learning that takes place in physical education lessons is different, and the types of problems leading to special needs may well be different, too. For this reason, Bailey and Robertson (2000) suggest that special educational needs in physical education should be framed within the context of *movement*.

A very useful framework for identifying pupils who have a special educational need in physical education is provided by Sugden and Wright (1996). They distinguish between pupils who have a special need that is *primarily described in terms of their movement skills*, and those who have a special need in physical education, but which is *secondary to other needs*. Included in the first category are pupils with physical disabilities, such as cerebral palsy or muscular dystrophy, as well as those with more general movement difficulties (sometimes called developmental co-ordination disorder (DCD) or dyspraxia). Conditions associated with the second category might be learning difficulties, sensory impairment, emotional and behavioural difficulties, attention deficit and hyperactivity disorder, and autism.

It is essential to understand that this is not a strict and precise classification, and that not every pupil experiencing one of these conditions will have a special need in physical education. Indeed, as is becoming clear with increased exposure to the Paralympic Games and other similar events, many people with disabilities or impairments are outstanding athletes. However, the framework serves to emphasize an important point: pupils' needs should be considered within specific contexts, rather than as a general statement about the child. To rephrase the last point: there is no such thing as a 'special needs pupil'; there are only 'pupils with special needs'. This distinction is much more than a semantic one.

With the previous cautions in mind, it is possible to outline some characteristics of certain conditions that may be associated with special needs in physical education. Detailed discussions of conditions is beyond the remit of this chapter, but there are a number of sources of further information, both about the condition in general and about specific teaching approaches within physical education, and these are indicated in the text. The reader is also directed to two excellent books for more information on this subject: Jowsey (1992) and Wright and Sugden (1999).

Some conditions associated with movement difficulties

Developmental co-ordination disorder (DCD) is a term used to describe movement difficulties of a kind not associated with a specific neurological disorder such as cerebral palsy. DCD is one of a cluster of names given to pupils with general movement problems; other names include dyspraxia, developmental dyspraxia, clumsiness, clumsy child syndrome, and disorder of attention, motor and perception (Robertson, 1999). Each of these labels refers to pupils whose movement skills are at functionally lower levels than those of their peers. The implications for physical education should be clear:

> Children with DCD acquire the basic skills of sitting, standing, walking, running, etc, but they may be delayed and they may have difficulty in using them flexibly to adapt to changing environmental demands. They can perform the skills at a rudimentary level, but they are less skilled than their peers, they have difficulty using the skills in context and often they look awkward. This often leads to a lack of participation in PE lessons and in play and recreational activities at break time.
> (Sugden and Wright, 1996: 115)

Cerebral palsy (CP) is a non-progressive disorder caused by early damage to the part of the brain responsible for movement. The degree of movement difficulty associated with CP varies considerably, from a slight problem with walking to very severe disability, and also from difficulty with only one limb to difficulty with all limbs (Bailey and Robertson, 2000). The brain damage that leads to CP may also lead to other difficulties, such as general learning difficulties, speech and language problems or epilepsy. However, some pupils with CP may be of normal or above average intelligence.

CP is characterized in a number of ways (see Sugden and Wright, 1996). One of the most relevant for teachers of physical education is in terms of the types of movements the individual performs. The most common form is labelled *spasticity*, and involves significantly increased muscle tone, and the occasional build-up and sudden release of tension. *Athetosis* is characterized by involuntary movements, such as spasms, writhing and twisting, and can also be accompanied by spastic actions. The third form, *ataxia*, is associated with postural instability and a stumbling walk.

Pupils with CP are likely to present some challenges to the teacher of physical education, but this does not mean that such pupils cannot take part in lessons alongside their peers. The teacher needs to be mindful of the different forms of CP, and the individual variations within each form, so it is advisable to talk to parents and the pupil about what the pupil is able to do in physical education lessons (this is a general principle when working with pupils with special needs). It may also be necessary to work with other professionals, like physiotherapists.

Spina bifida is a condition where one or more of the vertebral discs are not formed together. Sometimes, individuals with this condition have a protruding 'sac' containing either the coverings of the spinal cord or vertebrae. If there is damage to the spinal cord, the child may be paralysed: the higher the site of the damage, the more severe the disability. Some pupils with spina bifida may need to use wheelchairs, whilst others can walk with callipers and crutches. Within the context of physical education, the teacher needs to be aware that pupils with this condition can be insensitive to pain or damage to the legs. Some also have to wear a 'shunt', which is a device that drains off excess spinal fluid and can be knocked during vigorous games or gymnastic rolling activities.

Sensory impairment, whilst not a condition primarily associated with movement difficulties, can still have profound effects on pupils' experiences of physical activities and physical education. The term is used to describe hearing and visual difficulties (and it is worth remembering that pupils with these difficulties need not be completely deaf or blind). Our senses of hearing and sight provide much of the information we use to navigate ourselves around the world, so pupils with impairments can acquire movement difficulties as a consequence of their limited movement experiences. Vision, in particular, provides such a great deal of information on the environment around us, and also provides feedback on our actions, that a visual impairment can be very disadvantageous for developing children's movement ability.

Emotional and behavioural difficulties (EBD) occur with pupils who are withdrawn, hyperactive, aggressive or self-abusive, or have poor self-esteem. As such, EBD do not represent identifiable movement problems, but such difficulties may seriously interfere with learning movement skills. Conversely, pupils with EBD in some subjects may excel in physical education, and this should be acknowledged and recorded. Some pupils with EBD may have specific problems associated with a recognized condition, like *attention deficit and hyperactivity disorder* (ADHD) or *autistic spectrum disorders*, and teachers need to discuss with specialists and parents the possible implications of these with regard to the teaching and learning of physical education. (Strategies for addressing some behavioural problems are discussed in Chapter 6.)

These are just a proportion of the conditions associated with movement difficulties, either directly or indirectly, any one of which the teacher may experience in school. It is vital to remember that the pupil with special needs need not be disabled within an activity if there is appropriate and sensitive planning, teaching and assessment. However, if there is not, then that child can be further disabled by entering a spiral of failure. Ripley, Daines and Barrett (1997: 69) characterize this pattern of failure in this way:

1. The child finding an activity difficult – *is not motivated to do it.*
2. The child tries to avoid the activity – *does not attend, does something else, misbehaves, seeks attention.*
3. The child does not practise the activity – *and therefore finds it even harder to do it on other occasions.*

Task 7.1

Can you identify a pupil you are teaching who exhibits signs of entering into a 'spiral of failure'? What are the causes of this behaviour? What strategies can you employ to rectify the situation?

Discuss solutions with your mentor or other colleagues.

Inclusive physical education

'All PE lessons are by nature "mixed ability" sessions; an inclusive approach merely extends the parameters of the ability continuum' (Black and Haskins, 1996: 10).

The term 'special educational needs' was introduced as a more acceptable and useful alternative to earlier terms. The word 'handicap', for example, is of limited value to teachers, since it only provides a description of a condition, whilst a 'special need' is tied to a statement of the educational provision required. In recent years, however, some people have gone on to question the value of the term 'special educational needs', too, and have proposed the term 'inclusive education' instead. Perhaps this seems a mere rhetorical change, but advocates argue that the new terminology reflects a conviction that schools, like society, should be inclusive of the wide diversity of needs and abilities of pupils. An important statement of this conviction is provided by the Salamanca Statement of UNESCO (1994: 11):

> The fundamental principle of the inclusive school is that all children should learn together, wherever possible, regardless of any difficulties or differences they may have. Inclusive schools must recognize and respond to the diverse needs of their students, accommodating both different styles of learning and ensuring quality education to all through appropriate curricula, organizational arrangements, teaching strategies, resources use and partnership with their communities. There should be a continuum of special needs encountered by every school.

Within the United Kingdom, there is also a political commitment to a more inclusive educational system, as is outlined in the Green Paper *Excellence for All Children* (DfEE, 1997) and the consequent document *Meeting Special Educational Needs* (DfEE, 1998b), which states: 'There are strong educational, as well as social and moral grounds, for educating children with SEN, or with disabilities, with their peers. This is an important part of building an inclusive society. An increasing number of schools are showing that an inclusive approach can reinforce a commitment to higher standards for all' (DfEE, 1998b: 23).

These quotations are really saying two things: firstly, that the inclusion of pupils with special needs has a moral as well as practical dimension; secondly, that the effective development of such inclusive provision will be for the benefit of all pupils, not just those with special needs.

What does this mean for physical education? Perhaps the implications of these changes will be quite radical. Bailey and Robertson (2000) highlight just two consequences of a properly inclusive approach to physical education. First, teaching practices will need reshaping. Second, the organization of learning will have to become infinitely more flexible than it is at present. This chapter offers some suggestions for how this might be done.

Task 7.2

Barton (1993) has questioned whether the physical education curriculum that all pupils are entitled to access is premised on an enabling view of disability. He argues that important issues still need to be considered if all pupils are really going to participate on an equal basis with their able-bodied peers. He suggests that the following issues need to be considered:

- Physical education is the creation of and for able-bodied people.
- It gives priority to certain types of human movement.
- Individual success is viewed as a means of personal status and financial well-being. It is depicted as a way to the 'good life'.
- A whole consumer industry has been generated around such activities. Sport has become a commodity to be sold in the market place.
- The motivation to participate is encouraged through the articulations of idealized notions of 'normality'.

(Barton, 1993: 49)

- How do you respond to these charges against physical education and sport? In particular, focus on the first, second and final points of Barton's charge.
- Does physical education enforce a restricted notion of movement and normality? If so, is this avoidable?
- If the current form of the subject represents *exclusive* physical education, what might *inclusive* physical education look like?

Four principles should inform the planning and content of physical education for *all* pupils (DES/WO, 1991; see also Vickerman, 1997):

- *Entitlement*. All pupils have a right to participate fully in worthwhile activities.
- *Access*. This is achieved primarily by the provision of appropriate and challenging learning experiences and assessment mechanisms, allowing for modification when required.
- *Integration*. Pupils, even when following an adapted curriculum, should be doing so alongside their peers.
- *Integrity*. Physical education lessons should be demanding, motivating and exciting educationally.

According to this model, physical education needs to strike a balance between challenge and flexibility, between presenting pupils with sufficiently demanding activities and modifying those activities to reflect their individual needs and abilities. At the same time, it stresses a central principle of an inclusive physical education: wherever possible, pupils should be learning together.

Differentiation

'Special needs teaching is not something different and distinct from other forms of teaching, but is an extension of good professional practice' (Sugden and Wright, 1996: 121).

Teaching pupils with special needs or disabilities is not of a different character to teaching other pupils. Whilst there are important aspects of pupils' needs that should be considered in planning and teaching, the basic principles of good practice outlined in this book are the same for all pupils, although some aspects may require greater emphasis in certain situations. Of course, it is necessary to be aware of the character and implications of different conditions, and there may also be a need to liaise with other professionals, but this does not alter the educational role of the teacher.

Effective teaching requires that a range of teaching strategies, tasks and forms of organization is used to meet the different needs of the pupils in a class. This is often referred to as 'differentiation'. Differentiation involves 'recognising the variety of needs within a class, planning to meet needs, providing appropriate delivery and evaluation of the effectiveness of the activities in order to maximise the achievements of individual students' (NCET, 1993: 21).

According to inspection reports, differentiation is a particular weakness of newly qualified teachers. Her Majesty's Inspectorate (DES, 1988: 22) claimed that even in 'good' and 'excellent' lessons observed, there were still occasional weaknesses in 'differentiating the work so as to match the different levels of ability among pupils'. Similarly, OFSTED (1993: 24) reported that 'a lack of adequate differentiation was a feature of many lessons observed'.

There is some very useful guidance on differentiation in physical education (such as NCC, 1992 and Williams, 1996a). Perhaps the simplest approach is to distinguish between differentiation by task and by outcome. *Differentiation by task* occurs when the teacher plans and presents a number of different tasks of varying difficulty, and the pupils choose or are directed to the task that matches their ability level. *Differentiation by outcome* occurs when the teacher sets a challenge, and the pupils each answer that challenge according to their individual levels of ability (see Table 7.1).

Table 7.1 Differentiation by task and outcome (adapted from CCW, 1992)

Pupils plan and perform a gymnastic sequence in which weight must be taken on different body parts.	differentiation by task	– using only large body parts – using stable bases (eg two feet and one hand – using unstable bases (eg two hands) – inverted (eg bunny hop or shoulder stand or handstand)
	differentiation by outcome	– more challenging balances – clear shapes/better body awareness – variety of balances – greater control

The key to effective differentiation is planning. The difficulty for the trainee or newly qualified teacher is a lack of knowledge of the range of abilities of the pupils. This can be addressed, to some extent, by talking to previous teachers of the classes to be taught. There may be more information available on pupils with identified special needs. Ultimately, though, teachers need to make their own judgements about classes, and this comes from the experience of working with those classes. A useful approach during early lessons is to begin with tasks that are likely to challenge the majority ability range, but also plan adaptations to those tasks for higher and lower abilities, and intervene with them if it becomes clear that certain pupils need a different level of challenge. Increased familiarity with a class allows for more precise planning and differentiation.

Bailey (2000b) offers a framework for making decisions about differentiation in planning (see Figure 7.1).

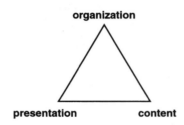

Figure 7.1   A model for differentiation

According to this model, the teacher makes a series of decisions that determine the character of the lesson. Each of the variables – organization, presentation and content – relates to a different aspect of the lesson. By making decisions about these variables, the teacher is in a position to differentiate to meet the needs of individuals or groups within a class.

Each of the variables can be further subdivided, to offer a range of differentiation strategies (see box below). These strategies need not involve a great deal of extra work for teachers. In fact, they are just the decisions a teacher must make in the planning of any lesson. The advantage of the approach suggested here is that these decisions are made explicitly and in a systematic manner.

Differentiation strategies

- *Organization*:
  - grouping;
  - space;
  - roles;
  - interaction.
- *Presentation*:
  - teaching style;
  - response;
  - resources;
  - support.
- *Content*:
  - task;
  - pace;
  - level;
  - practice style.

Organization variables

This refers to the social context of the learning. Decisions made regarding organization range from the character of pupil interaction – co-operative, competitive, individualistic – to the size of groups, and the use of the PE area.

Differentiation by grouping

There are numerous criteria for forming pupils into groups, such as ability, friendship or random groups (see Chapter 4). Broadly speaking, the smaller the group size, the easier it is for pupils to deal with the intellectual challenges presented to them: larger groups mean more choices and more decisions. It is often useful to allow pupils to work alone or in pairs when they are first introduced to a skill or concept, as this can present less pressure and give them greater space to explore and experiment.

Differentiation by space

Changing the amount of space allowed for the performance of a task can make it easier or more difficult. Some pupils with special needs, such as those using a wheelchair or with crutches, may need more space to turn or change direction, or simply for safety. Increasing the available space to play a game can offer the players more time to think and act, and decreasing it can make the game more challenging and quicker. It is also possible to divide the area up, and to restrict some players' movement around the playing area (as in netball). Specifying zones in which pupils must work makes decision making easier, and prevents a small number of players dominating the game. (Different ways of dividing up an area are presented in Chapter 4.)

Differentiation by roles

Many activities in physical education lessons involve a number of different roles. For example, a game of cricket might require the following: a bowler, two batters, many fielders and a wicketkeeper. It might also include umpires, coaches and a scorer. Ideally, all pupils will experience each of the roles, in order to build up a complete understanding of the game. However, pupils who are injured or who are otherwise unable to take part in the physical aspects of the lesson can still develop their knowledge and understanding by practising the other roles. One idea that has proved very successful when working with a class in which there is a pupil who is severely disabled is to give that pupil a specific, vital role within the game. For example, once a team scores during an invasion game, the pupil with a severe disability can try to 'convert' that goal by aiming a ball at a target.

Differentiation by interaction

Physical education tasks can be co-operative, competitive or individual. When a skill is being acquired, it is often worth while to allow pupils to practise without the extra pressure of competition. Some pupils with EBD can find competitive activities particularly stressful, and this can trigger misbehaviour. Of course, co-operative tasks can also present a challenge to some pupils, especially the young or pupils with autistic spectrum disorder, and may need gradual introduction. In planning lessons, therefore, the teacher needs to weigh up a series of factors, including pupils' ages, temperaments and the intended learning objectives.

Presentation variables

This refers to the way in which the curriculum is presented to pupils. It is important to consider the most effective form of presenting information, for supporting practice and of pupils showing their understanding.

Differentiation by teaching style

Different learning outcomes may demand different teaching styles. If the teacher is introducing a specific skill, especially if there is a safety principle involved, then a direct style may be most appropriate, where the skill is demonstrated and pupils attempt to reproduce it. On the other hand, if the teacher wants pupils to reflect on their performances or to consider a range of possible courses of actions, then more indirect styles may be more relevant. Also, pupils have their own preferred learning styles, and this means that they respond to some styles of teaching better than others.

Differentiation by response

Pupils can show their knowledge and understanding by demonstrating, speaking or writing, and as individuals, pairs or part of a group. The distinctively public nature of physical education means that some pupils may feel uncomfortable demonstrating their skills, but may be perfectly happy to explain their ideas to the teacher. Others may be happier showing their progress through performing as part of a group than as individuals.

Differentiation by resources

This category refers to pupils' use of equipment or apparatus. Changing resources can increase the difficulty of a task, or make it more manageable. For example, a pupil should practise gymnastic balances on the floor before progressing to apparatus, and should practise on apparatus with large surfaces before smaller surfaces. There are many different ways of varying the use of resources to meet the needs of pupils (see Table 7.2). An important factor in this regard is whether pupils are able to select their own resources, of if the teacher makes such decisions.

Table 7.2   Examples of differentiation by resources

Activity	Examples
Dance	– tempo, cadence and rhythm of music
Games	– size, weight and texture of ball – size of bat/racket – height of net – size of target/goal – length of handle – stationary or moving target
Gymnastics	– height of apparatus – area of apparatus
Swimming	– use of floats and armbands

Differentiation by support

Teachers can choose to use their time and that of any other adult helpers available in different ways. Sometimes extra help is needed for specific activities, as when giving support in gymnastics. At other times, individuals or groups may benefit from a little extra attention from the teacher, or from focused monitoring. Some pupils with statemented special needs may have a designated non-teaching assistant to support them, and teachers need to plan for the time of these assistants, as well as their own.

Content variables

This relates to the aspects of the curriculum that are to be developed during a lesson.

Differentiation by task

A common form of differentiation is to plan different tasks (or different versions of the same task) to match pupils' abilities or needs. Table 7.1 shows how a learning objective can solicit a number of tasks of different levels of difficulty.

Differentiation by pace

Pupils may progress through the planned activities at different rates. This may be a function of physical fitness, motivation or understanding. One way to plan for differentiation by pace is to provide work-cards for the different tasks in a lesson, and pupils progress through these cards at their own speed. Another way is to group pupils according to ability or fitness, and to extend the challenges presented to the more able or fitter groups, and give more time for the slower or less able groups.

Differentiation by level

Pupils can work at tasks at different levels of challenge. For example, athletics activities can be completed at different speeds, gymnastics skills can be performed with different levels of difficulty and games can be played with different sizes of teams. In each case, the differentiation takes place through the level of challenge presented to pupils.

Differentiation by practice style

Pupils may find it easier to attempt skills as a whole or as parts of the whole. For example, the basketball lay-up shot can be practised as a whole action, or it can be broken down into a run-up, a jump and a shot. Some pupils may succeed using the first approach, and others may prefer the second. Similarly, pupils at different stages of skill development need different types of practice. Those who have recently acquired the skill may benefit from small, repeated drills, those developing fluency may need sustained practice and those with a high level of skill may need to use the skill in an increasingly wider range of contexts.

Examples of the application of all the differentiation strategies are given in Table 7.3.

Table 7.3 Differentiation strategies, with examples of application

Strategy	Application
Differentiation by Grouping	*Swimming.* Pupils are divided into four groups by ability. Non-swimmers remain in the shallow end of the pool; higher-ability pupils use a lane for distance practice.
Differentiation by Space	*Relays.* Pupils using wheelchairs are given more space in a passing game, to allow for the greater area needed to turn and move.
Differentiation by Roles	*Outdoor adventurous activities.* For a problem-solving task, one pupil in a group directs, another is the judge and two others carry out the physical challenge. They then rotate roles.
Differentiation by Interaction	*Tennis.* Pupils new to the sport practise ball control skills individually, and then build up rallies co-operatively, before playing a simple competitive game.
Differentiation by Teaching Style	*Dance.* Very able pupils are encouraged to explore different ways of using stimuli for movement.
Differentiation by Response	*Gymnastics.* Injured pupil uses ICT to plan and represent a sequence of basic actions and linking actions.
Differentiation by Resources	*Softball.* Pupils are allowed to choose the size of bat, and to select whether to hit a moving or stationary ball.
Differentiation by Support	*Athletics.* A pupil with a visual impairment runs with a partner.
Differentiation by Task	*Dance.* Groups prepare a dance using different stimuli, such as music, poetry or natural sounds.
Differentiation by Pace	*Outdoor and adventurous activities.* Groups work through a series of tasks at their own rate.
Differentiation by Level	*Gymnastics.* Pupils perform headstand, with either tucked, straight or spread legs.
Differentiation by Practice Style	*Games.* Less able pupils practise short, repeated tasks, whilst the most able group learn to adapt and generalize the skills in new contexts.

Organizational strategies

Inclusive practices in physical education do not demand that all pupils participate at all times alongside their peers. Rather, they suggest that pupils should be included in lessons as far as is possible and in their best interests. The key here is flexibility of approach.

Black and Haskins (1996) propose an 'inclusion spectrum' methodology in addressing pupils' different needs in physical education. According to this view, there are five different approaches to the delivery and organization of an activity: mainstream, modified, parallel, adapted and separate:

- *Mainstream* activities are those in which everyone in the class is included, without adapting or modifying the activity.
- *Modified* activities involve the sorts of differentiation strategies discussed in the previous section – differentiated rules, space, equipment, roles and so on. Whilst there is differentiated or modified performance for pupils with different needs, all pupils work together on the same general task in the same area.
- *Parallel* activities are those in which pupils of different abilities are grouped together and participate in their own way, but in the same task. For example, able-bodied and wheelchair users might form two groups for games of volleyball.
- *Adapted* activities, or 'reverse integration', occur when all pupils take part in adapted tasks, or tasks that are specifically designed with disabled people in mind. For example, all pupils might play bocchia (an aiming game, rather like French petanque or bowls) together.
- *Separate* activities take place when a specific group of pupils practise an activity on their own. This might be in preparation for a competition, or for a movement assessment.

These approaches are summarized in Figure 7.2.

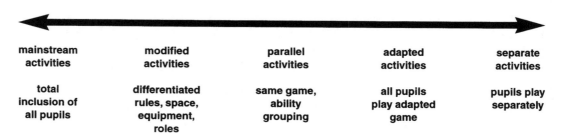

Figure 7.2 The inclusion spectrum (based on Black and Haskins, 1996)

Black (1999: 28) suggests that this approach can be used in different ways:

- Each approach can be adopted individually, and used as the main theme of the lesson.
- Two or more of the approaches can be utilized as part of a mixed-ability session.
- The whole group can progress through each approach in turn.

The approaches used will depend upon a range of factors, such as the task being undertaken, the ability level and range of the pupils, and the learning objectives of the lesson. Whatever the approach adopted, it is important not to be dogmatic about its use. There is no correct way, in absolute terms, only more or less appropriate ways in specific situations. The goal of inclusive practice is to meet the needs of all pupils. A flexible use of a range of strategies increases the likelihood that all pupils will be challenged and motivated, and that none will feel excluded from physical education.

Identifying and assessing special needs

The benefits of early identification and assessment of special educational needs are well established, and physical education is likely to have access to types of information about pupils that are not available to other teachers. The nature of the subject means that physical education teachers may be the first professionals to gather certain sorts of information, such as:

- movement difficulties;
- acquisition of basic physical skills;
- emotional and behavioural difficulties associated with an inability to handle competitive stress, accidental physical contact, failure and success;
- problems with getting dressed and undressed.

Other information may be more readily identifiable within the peculiar contexts of physical education, which may have remained hidden elsewhere, including:

- hearing and visual impairments;
- social isolation;
- language difficulties;
- signs of physical abuse.

The 1993 Education Act and the subsequent *Code of Practice on the Identification and Assessment of Special Educational Needs* (DFE, 1994) provide a detailed and systematic framework for identifying, assessing, planning and monitoring special educational needs. At the centre of the *Code of Practice* is a five-stage procedure, of which the first three stages relate to the school's internal procedures and the last two to those of the Local Education Authority (LEA). The end result of the five-stage process is usually the issuing of a 'statement of special educational needs' for the pupil, accompanied by some extra resources.

The five stages of the *Code of Practice* are outlined below, and summarized in Table 7.4:

- *Stage One* is the teacher's responsibility, and involves an initial statement of concern that a pupil is experiencing some difficulties in mainstream provision. At this stage, the action will usually involve an assessment by the teacher and, perhaps, an increase in the degree of differentiation offered. The teacher needs to pass the pupil's name to the school special educational needs co-ordinator (SENCO), who may decide to contact the parents, and who will review, with the teacher, the progress made by the pupil under the adapted provision.
- *Stage Two* is the joint responsibility of the teacher and the SENCO, and requires the formulation of an individual education plan (IEP), which describes in some detail the type of special need and the strategies being used to meet that need. The SENCO will work alongside the teacher, and together they will initiate a more detailed assessment of the pupil's needs to help with effective planning for that pupil. Progress will be reviewed, and a decision will be made regarding whether the pupil should remain at Stage Two, or has made sufficient progress to return to Stage One, or should move to Stage Three.
- *Stage Three* is mainly the responsibility of the SENCO, along with professionals from other agencies, such as educational psychologists, physiotherapists or GPs. A more thorough assessment of the pupil's needs will be carried out, and the SENCO will liaise closely with the teacher and parents to share information about the pupil's progress.

Table 7.4 Physical education and the Code of Practice

Stage One	– initial concern by teacher – teacher assessment – differentiation – progress reviewed
Stage Two	– SENCO registers pupil – teacher and SENCO draw up IEP and implement it – progress reviewed
Stage Three	– SENCO registers pupil – request for recognition that specialist support is required – consultation with other professionals – more thorough assessment – IEP revised and implemented – progress report
Stage Four	– multidisciplinary reports and assessments
Stage Five	– statement of special educational needs

- *Stage Four* is the school and LEA's responsibility. Reports from a range of interested parties (school, parents, educational psychologists, physiotherapists, social services and so on) may be requested by the LEA. Formal assessment of the pupil's needs is begun, and this may result in the issuing of a 'statement', and with it greater resource support for the pupil.
- *Stage Five* is the final phase of the procedure, and only relates to pupils with the most demanding special needs. At this stage, the LEA issues a statement, as well as extra money to the pupil. The school then has to implement the extra support and resources needed, as dictated by the statement. This is often in the form of a non-teaching assistant, or some specialist equipment.

Summary

This chapter has argued that physical education should adopt an inclusive approach to planning, teaching and assessment, based on differentiation, flexible lesson organization and commitment to integration. Key points to remember include the following:

- Teaching physical education to pupils with special educational needs is simply an extension of good practice.
- All pupils can benefit from physical education, and the teacher should be open to new approaches to increase inclusion and participation of the widest range of abilities in physical education lessons.
- There are numerous differentiation strategies, and these should be used selectively in planning and teaching.
- Pupils can experience physical education through a number of organizational approaches, from separate to fully inclusive activities.
- Teachers need to be familiar with the five-stage procedure outlined in the *Code of Practice*.

Further reading

Bailey, R P and Robertson, C R (2000) Including *all* pupils in primary school physical education, in *Teaching Physical Education 5–11*, ed R P Bailey and T M Macfadyen, Continuum, London

Jowsey, S (1992) *Can I Play Too? Physical education for physically disabled children in mainstream schools*, David Fulton, London

Wright, H and Sugden, D (1999) *Physical Education for All: Developing physical education in the curriculum for pupils with special educational needs*, David Fulton, London

8 Monitoring, assessment, recording, reporting and accountability

Introduction

There is virtually universal agreement among writers and policy makers that sound assessment lies at the very heart of effective teaching and learning. Since the advent of National Curricula in the United Kingdom, the role and importance of assessment and associated procedures have been continually highlighted. Yet, it is sometimes viewed as a source of concern for physical education teachers, and inspections reveal that it is a relatively weak feature of physical education provision (eg Clay, 1997; OHMCI, 1998), and one needing development and support. This chapter examines the role of assessment procedures in promoting pupils' learning in physical education, and offers approaches to assessing, recording and reporting pupil achievement that are simple, efficient and workable.

Objectives

By the end of this chapter you should:

- understand the nature and importance of monitoring, assessment, recording, reporting and accountability (MARRA), and especially ARR;
- be familiar with the key terms used in assessment;
- be able to draw upon a range of simple, effective strategies to assess pupils' learning and achievement.

Monitoring, assessment, recording, reporting and accountability

Monitoring, assessment, recording, reporting and accountability (MARRA) is a relatively new phrase in the teacher's lexicon, and refers to that cluster of activities concerned with assessing pupils' learning and achievement. Trainee and newly qualified teachers are required to demonstrate their ability to carry out these activities to nationally defined standards (DfEE, 1998a; TTA, 2000a).

What is MARRA?

MARRA stands for:

- **M**onitoring – effectively overviewing and analysing the learning environment.
- **A**ssessment – closer examination of pupils' learning and achievement as a result of a lesson or unit of work.
- **R**ecording – keeping track of areas identified by monitoring and assessment, including the attainment of the learning objectives to assist further planning and reporting.
- **R**eporting – informing others about the learning and achievement that have taken place.
- **A**ccountability – evaluation by others of the organization by analysing the results of assessment.

As can be seen, all aspects of MARRA relate to assessment, and assessment is inextricably linked to pupil learning. This chapter examines the different elements of MARRA in some detail, and considers the ways in which they each contribute to pupil learning and achievement. 'Accountability' refers to schools' responsibilities towards pupils, parents and other members of society in their delivery of an appropriate and effective education programme, and, as such, has moral, legal and financial dimensions. The personal levels of accountability for the teacher are stressed throughout this book. The wider levels associated with schools and education authorities are outside the remit of this book, and so will not be discussed in detail (see Headington, 2000, for a fuller coverage).

Monitoring

Headington (2000: 8) defines monitoring as 'the skill of being able to have a constant, clear and accurate overview of pupils within a learning situation and environment'. As was emphasized in Chapter 3, the 'busy, happy and good' syndrome, in which pupils appear to be actively involved in the lesson but where their actual learning is rather slight, should caution teachers to attend to pupils' skills, knowledge and understanding in a systematic way. Monitoring is the way in which this information is gathered.

If monitoring is to contribute to learning, the teacher needs to be clear about the things pupils are supposed to be learning during a lesson or unit. In other words, monitoring should be informed by an awareness of the learning objectives contained within the lesson plan or unit of work. If it is, the teacher will be in a position to judge the extent to which pupils have achieved the intended learning objectives of the lesson or unit, and can make an informed decision about whether to extend, adapt or abandon the task being undertaken.

Much guidance of monitoring and assessment stresses the importance of basing judgements on fact, not speculation, and with reference to readily identifiable evidence of attainment. However, things are not quite as simple as they might first appear. As was discussed in Chapter 2, some learning objectives are not easily assessed, as they cannot be witnessed directly by the teacher. This is true of a great deal of learning in physical education, such as understanding, attitudes, feelings and values. How can these sorts of learning be monitored and assessed? Some forms of learning can be 'translated' into more readily observable forms. For example, understanding of tactical awareness in an invasion game can be partially assessed by observing the way pupils perform within a game. Sometimes, though, the monitoring of things like understanding or feelings can only be done by talking with individual pupils, by asking them divergent questions and by building up a picture of their understanding or feelings through a series of observations.

A related problem concerns the nature of physical skill learning. Once a skill has been acquired, there is a need to practise that skill to provide a degree of fluency and proficiency. After that, pupils may be required to apply the same skill in a variety of situations. At this stage, pupils are not learning new techniques, but are simply learning to perform their existing techniques *better* (Haring *et al*, 1978). Pupils may become demotivated in these situations, as they stop seeing obvious progress. This can be helped by monitoring and assessing for effort as well as achievement. Nicholls (1995: 227) makes a similar point, and raises further issues for consideration regarding monitoring:

> If the outcomes of learning are judged solely by the amount of information retrieved from a pupil then the importance of the quality of thinking has been ignored. It is possible to differentiate quality of pupil response by the extent to which the information given has been transferred and transformed by the pupils, ie, that they are able to demonstrate understanding.

Much of the content of earlier chapters is of relevance here. Effective monitoring demands that the teacher is aware of pupils' learning, as well as any difficulties, as they carry out the various activities of the lesson. It also means that teachers need to interact continually with learners, through focused interventions, questioning, discussions and observations, if they are to develop a full and accurate picture of the pupils' issues. It is insufficient simply to judge whole groups; monitoring should be used to gain information about individuals and their specific issues. Some teachers use informal systems, such as notebooks to record their observations of pupils' successes and problems, to support their monitoring, and to feed into their assessment and planning systems (see Table 8.1).

Pupils can also be encouraged to monitor their own work. By sharing lesson objectives with pupils at the beginning of the lesson and referring to them when relevant, the teacher can help pupils evaluate their own performances and those of their peers. This can help pupils understand the context and meaning of the tasks in which they are engaged, which, in turn, can promote motivation and understanding. This can be further developed by discussing achievement in the concluding phase of the lesson and negotiating future lesson objectives.

Table 8.1 An example of an informal monitoring system (written in an exercise book)

Activity/ Date	Class	Observation	Action
Tennis 7/3	9B	Many pupils seem to be having difficulty with serve – accuracy and control.	Differentiated tasks for next lesson.
Gymnastics 9/3	7T	All demonstrated control and fluency in basic rolls.	Introduce different entry and exit positions for rolls.
Dance 13/3	8C	Excellent understanding of process of composition.	Plan more challenging compositional task for next week – variety of stimuli?

Assessment

'Assessment is not necessarily integral to all teaching, but it is integral to good or effective teaching and learning' (Piotrowski, 2000: 51).

Assessment in education is concerned with obtaining and interpreting information about pupils' skills, knowledge and understanding, and their learning needs. As such, it resembles closely the monitoring element of MARRA (discussed above). Assessment is more specific than monitoring: where monitoring generally provides the teacher with an overview of the learning of the class as a whole, assessment provides much more detailed information about the learning and achievement of individuals, specifically as they relate to the learning objectives of the lesson or the unit of work. Also, as Carroll (1994) argues persuasively, assessment always involves making a *judgement*. Assessment does not simply note what pupils have done in a lesson, but also makes some sort of qualitative statement as well.

Assessment should focus upon *what* pupils learn and *how well* they learn it. This information becomes the basis for future planning and target setting, and provides teachers with valuable feedback to their own performances as teachers. Assessment is part of a cycle of planning, teaching, learning and assessment (see Figure 8.1), in which teachers make judgements of pupils' performance, which inform future planning, which directs their teaching and, in turn, affects pupils' performance.

Purposes of assessment

Nicholls (1999b) suggests that there are three fundamental reasons for assessment: feedback, progress and motivation. *Feedback* provides information about pupils' progress, which allows teachers to evaluate the effectiveness of their teaching by

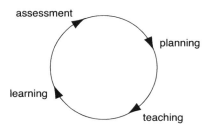

Figure 8.1 The plan–teach–learn–assess cycle

assessing how well the learning objectives have been achieved. It also gives direct feedback to pupils, by comparing their performance with their previous 'best', class performance or national expectations. Assessment also provides vital information on pupils' *progress*. This information helps the teacher address pupils' learning needs, and feeds into recording and reporting procedures (discussed later in this chapter). Finally, assessment is a key factor in encouraging pupils to strive to succeed and improve their skills, knowledge and understanding, and as such is an effective mechanism for future improvement and *motivation*.

Other purposes of assessment in physical education include:

- assisting planning for differentiation;
- helping pupils diagnose their own strengths and weaknesses;
- to select for a specific purpose, eg school teams;
- to discriminate between pupils, eg A levels;
- identifying learning or movement difficulties;
- certification, eg National Governing Body awards.

Principles of assessment

In order to make a fair and appropriate assessment, the teacher needs to adhere to certain principles of good practice. Carroll (1994) proposes the following four principles as fundamental to effective assessment in physical education:

- validity;
- reliability;
- objectivity;
- clear criteria.

Assessment is *valid* if it measures what it says it measures. The most valid forms of assessment are those that are as close as possible to the actual situation being assessed. The best, perhaps only, way to assess a child's performance in gymnastics is to get that child to do some gymnastics; written tests are unsuitable, as they assess different skills. A judgement is *reliable* if it provides the same finding under the same conditions on different occasions (Piotrowski, 2000). Making a reliable assessment involves an appreciation of the factors that can influence performance, such as the context of the assessment, the standards applied in assessing and sheer luck. Assessments should also be *objective*, in that they should not reflect personal bias. The most common forms of bias are of gender, ethnicity and social background. Finally, assessments should involve the use of *clear criteria*. Vague and ill-defined criteria are useless, since they always involve some doubt that they have actually been achieved.

One more principle could be added to Carroll's list: assessment should always be *practical*. Assessment procedures that are valid, reliable, objective and involve clear criteria, but which are also massively time-consuming or which take the teacher away from proper supervision of the lesson, are not advisable. The challenge for teachers of physical education is to find a system of assessment that fulfils the principles of good practice without preventing them from carrying out their other responsibilities.

The language of assessment

Part of the difficulty facing trainee and newly qualified teachers when approaching assessment is that of language: they have to acquire a whole new vocabulary of assessment terms. Although initially off-putting, the terminology of assessment is relatively easy to master. Table 8.2 summarizes some of the key terms, and offers some examples in physical education.

What to assess?

Before the introduction of the 2000 version of the National Curriculum for physical education, there were frequent complaints that teachers were given little guidance regarding what pupils of different abilities ought to be learning and hence what teachers should be assessing (eg Wetton, 1988). Now, however, there is a framework from which learning objectives (and therefore assessment criteria) can be drawn (see Table 8.3).

The level descriptions provide the basis on which to make judgements about pupils' performance at the end of Key Stages 1, 2 and 3. At Key Stage 4, the level descriptions can be used to assess attainment and progress, alongside national qualifications like GCSEs and GNVQs. In deciding the level of attainment at the end of each Key Stage, teachers need to judge which description best fits each pupil's performance. The range of levels and the expected attainment within each stage are outlined in Table 8.4.

The stages of development, themselves, are not sufficient to act as learning objectives (and hence criteria for assessment). Reference also needs to be made to the Programmes of Study (see Chapter 1), which add information on the types of activities pupils ought to be undertaking. From these two sources of statutory guidance, it is possible to select learning objectives and assessment criteria for lesson plans and units of work, which, in turn, can inform decisions regarding lesson content.

Table 8.2 The language of assessment

Assessment Term	Meaning	Physical Education Examples
Formative Assessment	ongoing assessment that takes place during the learning process, and involves describing progress, giving pupils constructive feedback and identifying pupils' future learning needs	offering pupils an evaluation of their performance, along with suggestions for improvement
Summative Assessment	assessment at the end of a specified period (such as a unit of work), which identifies the standard of attainment achieved by an individual	A level written examinations at the end of the course
Criteria Referenced Assessment	assessment of whether or not a pupil can do a specific task or set of tasks	National Governing Body awards NC expectation that all pupils can swim unaided over a distance of 25 metres
Norm Referenced Assessment	assessment of an individual's performance in relation to that of others in the group	testing all the pupils in a class in running or swimming, and recording their times; then dividing the class into ability groups for differentiated teaching
Ipsative Referenced Assessment	comparing pupils' current and previous performances	individuals record scores from a fitness circuit, and attempt to beat their own personal best in future sessions
Internal Assessment	assessment devised and carried out by the teacher as part of his or her own teaching programme	teacher's notes of groups' performance of basic skills at the start of a unit of work, which are used to inform future planning and teaching in the unit
External Assessment	devised by external groups, such as examination boards and National Governing Bodies	GCSEs, GNVQs, A levels in physical education/sports studies
Informal Assessment	assessment that takes place as part of the normal PE lesson	teacher observes performance and makes notes of individuals or groups for future planning
Formal Assessment	assessment made following prior warning to allow pupils to prepare	the assessment of a gymnastics sequence at the end of a unit of work

Table 8.3 Attainment targets for physical education

Level	Acquiring and Developing Skills	Selecting and Applying Skills	Evaluating and Improving Skills	Developing Knowledge and Understanding of Fitness and Health
1	Pupils copy, repeat and explore simple skills and actions with basic control and co-ordination.	They start to link these skills and actions in ways that suit the activities.	They describe and comment on their own and others' actions.	They talk about how to exercise safely, and how their bodies feel during an activity.
2	Pupils explore simple skills. They copy, remember, repeat and explore simple actions with control and co-ordination.	They vary skills, actions and ideas, and link these in ways that suit the activities. They begin to show some understanding of simple tactics and basic compositional ideas.	They talk about differences between their own and others' performance and suggest improvements.	They understand how to exercise safely, and describe how their bodies feel during different activities.
3	Pupils select and use skills, actions and ideas appropriately, applying them with co-ordination and control.	They show that they understand tactics and composition by starting to vary how they respond.	They can see how their work is similar to and different from others' work, and use this understanding to improve their own performance.	They give reasons why warming up before an activity is important, and why physical activity is good for their health.
4	Pupils link skills, techniques and ideas, and apply them accurately and appropriately.	Their performance shows precision, control and fluency, and that they understand tactics and composition.	They compare and comment on skills, techniques and ideas used in their own and others' work, and use this understanding to improve their performance.	They explain and apply basic safety principles in preparing for exercise. They describe what effects exercise has on their bodies, and how it is valuable to their fitness and health.
5	Pupils select and combine their skills, techniques and ideas and apply them accurately and appropriately, consistently showing precision, control and fluency.	When performing, they draw on what they know about strategy, tactics and composition.	They analyse and comment on skills and techniques and how these are applied in their own and others' work. They modify and refine skills and techniques to improve their performance.	They explain how the body reacts during different types of exercise, and warm up and cool down in ways that suit the activity. They explain why regular, safe exercise is good for their fitness and health.
6	Pupils select and combine skills, techniques and ideas.	They apply them in ways that suit the activity, with consistent precision, control and fluency.	They analyse and comment on how skills, techniques and ideas have been used in their own and	They explain how to prepare for, and recover from, the activities. They explain how different types of

Table 8.3 *continued*

Level	Acquiring and Developing Skills	Selecting and Applying Skills	Evaluating and Improving Skills	Developing Knowledge and Understanding of Fitness and Health
		When planning their own and others' work, and carrying out their own work, they draw on what they know about strategy, tactics and composition in response to changing circumstances, and what they know about their own and others' strengths and weaknesses.	others' work, and on compositional and other aspects of performance, and suggest ways to improve.	exercise contribute to their fitness and health, and describe how they might get involved in other types of activities and exercise.
7	Pupils select and combine advanced skills, techniques and ideas, adapting them accurately and appropriately to the demands of the activities. They consistently show precision, control, fluency and originality.	Drawing on what they know of the principles of advanced tactics and compositional ideas, they apply these in their own and others' work. They modify them in response to changing circumstances and other performers.	They analyse and comment on their own and others' work as individuals and team members, showing that they understand how skills, tactics or composition and fitness relate to the quality of the performance. They plan ways to improve their own and others' performance. They explain the principles of practice and training, and apply them effectively.	They explain the benefits of regular, planned activity on health and fitness, and plan their own appropriate exercise and activity programme.
8	Pupils consistently distinguish and apply advanced skills, techniques and ideas, consistently showing high standards of precision, control, fluency and originality.	Drawing on what they know of the principles of advanced tactics or composition, they apply these principles with proficiency and flair in their own and others' work. They adapt them appropriately in response to changing circumstances and other performers.	They evaluate their own and others' work, showing that they understand the impact of skills, strategy and tactics or composition, and fitness on the quality and effectiveness of performance. They plan ways in which their own and others' performance could be improved. They create action plans and ways of monitoring improvement.	They use their knowledge of health and fitness to plan and evaluate their own and others' exercise and activity programme.

Table 8.3 *continued*

Level	Acquiring and Developing Skills	Selecting and Applying Skills	Evaluating and Improving Skills	Developing Knowledge and Understanding of Fitness and Health
Exceptional Performance	Pupils consistently use advanced skills, techniques and ideas with precision and fluency.	Drawing on what they know of the principles of advanced strategies and tactics or composition, they consistently apply these principles with originality, proficiency and flair in their own and others' work.	They evaluate their own and others' work, showing that they understand how skills, strategy and tactics or composition, and fitness relate to and affect the quality and originality of performance. They reach judgements independently about how their own and others' performance could be improved, prioritizing aspects for further development.	They consistently apply appropriate knowledge and understanding of health and fitness in all aspects of their work.

Table 8.4 Levels of attainment through the Key Stages (from http://www.nc.uk.net/about/about_ pe.html)

Range of Levels within which the Great Majority of Pupils are Expected to Work		Expected Attainment for the Majority of Pupils at the End of the Key Stage	
Key Stage 1	1–3	At age 7	2
Key Stage 2	2–5	At age 11	4
Key Stage 3	3–7	At age 14	5/6

Task 8.1

Selecting a Key Stage of your choice, and with reference to the Programmes of Study and the eight-stage attainment target for physical education, devise a set of learning objectives for individual lessons in the following activity areas:

- games;
- gymnastics;
- dance;
- swimming.

The learning objectives should be reasonable for a child in the selected Key Stage to achieve *by the end of the lesson*.

Once you have done this, list an assessment criterion for each of the learning objectives. How will you know that the pupils have achieved these objectives? What sort of evidence could there be of attainment?

Methods of assessment

It has been argued that assessment should not be restricted to easily observable, behavioural features of pupils' skills, knowledge and understanding. Rather, teachers should aim to build up a picture of pupils' ranges of abilities through a variety of assessment methods. Informal methods of assessment largely rely on ongoing observation and verbal interaction. More formal methods, like focused demonstrations or written tasks, will usually take place at the end of a unit of work, year or Key Stage. The key factors in determining the best assessment procedures at a given time are validity, reliability and practicality. Therefore, the teacher needs to be very clear about the aspects of learning to be assessed.

Traditionally, physical education teachers have drawn on a rather narrow range of evidence in support of the assessment of pupils. It need not be just the teacher who gathers evidence of attainment. Pupils, even very young children, can become involved in the process of assessment, and this can significantly contribute to their own understanding. As SEAC (1992) point out: 'Teacher assessment can help pupils to understand what they are learning and to chart their own progress. Pupils can be actively involved in their own assessment: reviewing their work and progress; setting future targets for learning; and deciding, in discussion with the teacher, which pieces of work provide evidence of particular attainments.'

Self and peer assessment offer interesting ways of gathering evidence. However, these are not skills that all pupils will have developed naturally, and the teacher will need to introduce them gradually, making sure that all assessment is fair, positive and sensitive. Some schools go even further, and translate the statutory statements of attainment for pupils in a form that they can understand and use, and these are often pinned on a PE noticeboard, along with pictorial examples of the activity areas from the Programmes of Study (Mawer, 1995).

Williams (1996b) identifies some of the range of possible methods of assessment in physical education:

- observation of performance;
- pupil self-assessment;
- peer assessment;
- written materials;
- group discussions;
- answers to questions;
- pupils' explanations or descriptions.

Task 8.2

Identify the sorts of information from physical education that can be gathered by the different methods of assessment outlined above.

Spackman (1998: 7) argues that 'a good assessment policy can be readily applied to working documentation, such as units of work, and subsequently used in the teaching situation to support pupil learning. An ineffective policy is one which in some way is "bolted on" to units of work and has little application in the teaching situation itself.' She suggests a simple and effective way of doing this: numbering the learning objectives in units of work (she calls them 'outcomes') and marking the relevant number in the assessment column opposite an activity through which the objective might be achieved.

Task 8.3

Draft two units of work, with different activity area themes, using the assessment procedure outlined above. Discuss your units of work with your mentor, and consider ways of developing the unit:

- Do the assessment points offer valid and reliable sources of information on pupils' performance and learning?
- Are *all* of the learning objectives related to assessment points?
- Do the learning activities offer genuine opportunities to gain evidence of attainment?

If possible, deliver one of the units of work. When you evaluate at the end of the unit, focus particularly on your assessment of pupils' performance and learning.

Recording

Every physical education teacher needs to maintain records of pupils' attainment in the subject. Fortunately, there is no need to compile extensive or elaborate documents, and the emphasis should always be on records that are simple and manageable. Records should focus on pupils' learning in relation to the National Curriculum for physical education, and indicate their attainment with regard to the learning objectives of the units of work they have undertaken, as well as broader cross-curricular themes (ICT, citizenship, literacy and numeracy).

Records fulfil a number of functions, that is to:

- aid remembering of pupils' achievements;
- inform planning and differentiation;
- highlight causes for concern with individual pupils;
- act as a basis from which reports can be made;
- communicate information with other teachers;
- ensure continuity from year to year;
- chart rates of progress;
- compare pupils;
- provide evidence for accountability purposes.

It should be clear from this list that, whilst records for physical education should be simple and workable, they should also be detailed enough to satisfy many functions.

There are numerous examples of recording for physical education (see, for example, Carroll, 1994; Headington, 2000; Piotrowski, 2000). One example is provided in Figure 8.2.

KS/YEAR: UNIT:	Learning Objectives of Unit: 1. 2. 3.				
Pupil Names	Acquiring and Developing Skills	Selecting and Applying Skills	Evaluating and Improving Skills	Knowledge and Understanding of Fitness and Health	Comments

Figure 8.2 Example recording sheet

This recording system is for completion by the teacher at the end of a unit of work. References to the attainment of the learning objectives can be included under one of the strands of the attainment target for physical education, as can identification of the level achieved. It is important to include some qualitative information, so the comment boxes allow the teacher to personalize the records for each pupil assessed.

In the past, many schools have relied upon National Governing Body awards schemes as the basis for their record keeping for physical education. Whilst these schemes have some uses, they are inadequate as a foundation for an effective record-keeping system. Records should reflect the learning undertaken during the unit or year, and for this reason cannot just be taken 'off the shelf': they need to be focused upon the planned unit and its learning objectives.

Reporting

Reporting is the part of the assessment process that deals with communicating pupils' attainment and learning needs to interested groups. It can be either formative, offering information that can be useful to support further teaching and learning, or summative, providing information about pupils' attainment at a given point. Headington (2000) states that there are three main audiences for reporting: pupils, parents and other professionals. All three groups have shared needs, such as a demand for evidence of achievement rather than mere speculation. They also have differences. The most obvious of these is that the different groups are likely to have quite different understandings of the content, context and language of attainment. Therefore, it is necessary for the teacher to adapt the reporting output for these different audiences.

Within the context of physical education, Clay (1997: 9) has noted that 'reports are most often simple with details of activities covered and attitudes adopted rather than focusing on achievement and skill development'. Spackman (1998) has suggested that the majority of the report should be taken up with evidence of pupils' attainment and progress. This should focus upon the learning that has taken place as part of the units of work experienced during the year.

Similar principles to those discussed earlier in this chapter apply to reporting. Reports should be:

- accurate;
- based on evidence;
- focused upon pupil learning and attainment;
- useful to the reader;
- economical in terms of the teacher's time and preparation.

Piotrowski (2000) suggests that effective report writing can be accomplished by basing the pupil's report on that pupil's records. In other words, the information that has been collected as part of the normal record keeping can simply be translated into a narrative about the pupil's work and achievement during the year. This will include details of levels reached within the attainment target, learning objectives attained and a target for future work.

Task 8.4

Select three pupils from your class, and write a report of 60 words on each. Base your reports on your experiences with the pupils so far, if you have not taught them for a year. Make sure you include reference to levels reached, learning objectives attained and a target for future attainment.

Show your reports to your mentor, and discuss ways in which they can be improved.

Summary

Monitoring, assessment, recording, reporting and accountability are inextricably linked to pupils' learning and achievement, and deserve great attention. The key points to remember from this chapter include:

- Teachers should aim to gather information on pupils' learning from a range of sources, including their own monitoring and observations, pupils' performance, peer and self-assessment, and questioning.
- Records should offer a balance of relevant detail and ease of use.
- Reports should present information on pupil achievement, including qualitative statements about individuals' progress.

Further reading

Carroll, B (1994) *Assessment in Physical Education: A teacher's guide to the issues*, Falmer, London

Headington, R (2000) *Monitoring, Assessment, Recording, Reporting and Accountability*, David Fulton, London

Piotrowski, S (2000), Assessment, recording and reporting, in *Teaching Physical Education 5–11*, ed R P Bailey and T M Macfadyen, Continuum, London

9 Information and communication technology

Introduction

Computers and other information technologies are fast becoming accepted as normal parts of both society and schooling. Children at the start of the 21st century are habituated to high levels of stimulation, they are visually aware, steeped in a culture of rapidly moving images and sounds, and are often adept with modern technology beyond the level of many adults (Martyn, 1999). There is a growing recognition that schools need to capitalize on this technical sophistication, and build upon it in the education of pupils for a rapidly changing world. Moreover, there is an expectation for teachers in all subjects to exploit the potential of these technologies to support teaching and learning. This chapter considers the role of information and communication technology within the context of physical education, and suggests ways in which its enormous potential can be of benefit to both teachers and pupils.

Objectives

By the end of this chapter you should:

- understand recent policies in information and communication technology;
- appreciate the implications for your teaching of physical education;
- have a range of ideas for utilizing information and communication technology to support teaching and learning in physical education lessons;
- know how to locate further information and guidance for the use of information and communication technology in physical education.

The relationship between physical education and information and communication technology

As information and communication technology (ICT) becomes an increasingly central feature of school life, it is becoming evident that its use within physical education lessons is not keeping up with that in other subjects (Conway, 2000). Part of the reason for this seems to be that physical education is viewed as essentially a 'physical' or 'practical' subject, less suited to ICT use than more sedentary aspects of the curriculum. This is Fox's (undated: 1) concern:

> Clearly, this view is built on the assumption that the only means of learning in physical education is through the process of taking part in physical activity; cognitive processes take on a minor role. In this political climate, the scope for Information Technology in the learning process seems very limited. The problem is similar to the difficulties that have already been faced in trying to establish the use of lessons involving written work, text-books or audio-visual aids as a mode of learning in PE. Where the view predominates that PE should be restricted exclusively to the use of movement as its educational medium, with the playing field or sports hall providing its location, Information Technology innovation is likely to be difficult to achieve.

Nevertheless, the inclusion of ICT within physical education is a statutory requirement at Key Stages 3 and 4, and is viewed as good practice in the primary phase, as part of the principle that it is good practice to be able to draw upon as wide a range of teaching strategies as possible in the promotion of pupil learning. Trainee teachers are also expected to develop a suitable level of understanding to 'be able to exploit the potential of ICT to meet their teaching objectives' (TTA, 2000b). This chapter argues that ICT offers new opportunities for learning and the development of understanding, and should be considered a fundamental part of the teacher's toolkit.

Task 9.1

What is your view of the relationship between PE and ICT?

Using the Internet, access Kenneth Fox's online article, 'A sporting chance for Information Technology?' (http://www.rice.edn.deakin.edu.au/Archives/DITTE/d55.htm):

- What are the main barriers to greater use of ICT in PE?
- What does the notion of PE being a 'practical' subject mean, in terms of curriculum planning and teaching?
- Would the way PE is taught need to change to allow greater implementation of ICT's potential?
- The exercise sciences rely heavily upon ICT. How might this be reflected in physical education?
- Is the age of pupils a factor in the implementation of ICT in PE?

What is information and communication technology?

It is important to distinguish between information technology (IT) and information and communication technology (ICT). IT is 'the design, study and use of processes for representing physical, hypothetical or human relationships employing the collection, creation, storing, retrieving, manipulation, presentation, sending and receiving of information' (Cox, 1999: 60). ICT, on the other hand, refers to the use of these technological tools to support pupils' learning. So, ICT is distinct from (but reliant upon) IT: it is much more than simply learning to use modern technology; it involves the promotion of learning through that technology.

The range of technological tools available to the physical education teacher is vast, and might include the following:

- radio;
- television;
- tape recorders;
- video recorders;
- CD players;
- stopwatches and other timing devices;
- calculators;
- heart-rate monitors;
- digital blood-pressure machines;

- cameras – analogue, digital, video;
- personal computers (laptops and desktops);
- scanners;
- fax machines;
- Internet;
- intranet;
- e-mail;
- videoconferencing.

Most of these are readily available in schools, and can be used by teachers to enhance their teaching and to support the learning of pupils in different ways.

Computers and audio-visual aids have been used in schools for many years, but it is only relatively recently that policy makers have placed such great attention on ICT's central place within the school and the curriculum. In 1998, for example, the government announced a series of new programmes amounting to over £1.2 billion, towards the National Grid for Learning (NGfL), ICT for all teacher trainees and an ICT training allocation for all practising teachers (Cox, 1999). The NGfL has been a particularly high-profile development related to the increased use of ICT in schools. It has been described as 'a way of finding and using online learning and teaching materials' and 'a mosaic of interconnecting networks and education services based on the internet' (DfEE, 1998c), and aims to have all schools connected by 2002, with 75 per cent of teachers and 50 per cent of pupils having their own e-mail addresses and file space by that date (see http://www.dfee.gov.uk/grid/challenge/index.htm).

Guidance material for ICT relevant to physical education teachers is rather sparse and soon outdated, in comparison with other foundation subjects, and the Teacher Training Agency's (TTA, 2000b) expectations for trainee teachers' knowledge and understanding of ICT are probably the most thorough and useful guide available, even for experienced teachers. This document is available at: http://www.canteach.gov.uk/info/itt/supporting/ict-exemp.htm. A summary of the ways in which ICT has the potential to make a significant contribution to teaching and learning in physical education is outlined in the box below (based on TTA, 2000b).

ICT has the potential to make a significant contribution at every stage of physical education, for example to:

- *improve pupils' skills and techniques*, eg by using video to demonstrate to pupils the correct way to perform a stroke in swimming or a particular technique in athletics;
- *help pupils review, evaluate and improve their own performance*, eg by video-taping and reviewing composition in dance, sequences in gymnastics, and strategies and tactics in games;

- *develop pupils' understanding and knowledge of the subject*, eg by viewing CD ROMs or videos of high-quality performances in sport;
- *shift time*, eg by using slow motion, *and space*, eg by viewing the same technique from different angles, so that pupils can appreciate the details of movement exemplified above;
- *develop pupils' understanding of the human body, physiology and health education*, eg by monitoring heart rate against different types of physical activity.

ICT has the potential to offer valuable support to the PE teacher, for example by:

- *helping to locate good examples of performance* for demonstration or teaching that will help pupils to set appropriate targets;
- *supporting them in the administration* associated with, for example:
  - arranging sporting fixtures, eg by e-mail;
  - grouping and regrouping pupils;
  - compiling lists and information, eg team sheets or sports reports;
  - scoring and recording;
  - assessing and recording pupil performance.

Good practice in the use of ICT

Teachers sometimes feel under pressure to include ICT in their lessons, and this can express itself in rather awkward or tenuous content. The overriding principle is that ICT should positively contribute to pupils' learning, and not detract from it. If there is a danger of ICT getting in the way of learning, it should not be used. This is one benefit, at least, of physical education's peripheral position in the ICT guidance: we can be even more selective in our use of the technology than our colleagues can!

Beashel and Sibson (2000: 7) summarize the situation nicely when they say, 'ICT is not a replacement for good quality teaching. Used sensibly however it can make good lessons better.' This is also the position underlying the TTA's (2000b) three key principles of the effective use of ICT:

1. Decisions about when, when not and how to use ICT in lessons should be based on whether the use of ICT supports good practice in teaching the subject. If it does not, it should not be used.
2. In planning and in teaching, decisions about when, when not and how to use ICT in a particular lesson or sequence of lessons must be directly related to the teaching and learning objectives in hand.

3. The use of ICT should either allow the trainee or the pupil to achieve something that could not be achieved without it; or allow the trainee to teach or the pupils to learn something more effectively and efficiently than they could otherwise; or both.

In other words, the use of ICT should arise *naturally* within the process of planning and delivering lessons, and should not be considered an add-on or alternative to normal teaching.

To elucidate how this natural use of ICT can be included within normal physical education lessons, consider two brief case studies. These are based on observations of real lessons, working with pupils in Key Stages 1 and 3. The ICT applications have been highlighted in each case. (An example of the use of ICT in a GCSE physical education lesson is provided in TTA, 2000b.)

Case study 1: Key Stage 1 (Year 2)

Learning objective/National Curriculum reference

'For pupils to recognize and describe how their bodies feel during different activities.'

Summary of lesson content

This lesson was part of a cross-curricular project on 'Our bodies'. In this lesson, the children engaged in a variety of activities, and recorded how they felt after each one.

The teacher used a *word processor* and *clip art* to prepare a series of work-cards to show the different activities. Each sheet contained a word and a simple picture to represent the action. At the start of the lesson, the teacher showed the class each card, and asked individuals to demonstrate the actions:

- run (jog on the spot);
- balance (walk along a marking on the floor);
- catch (in pairs, with a large ball);
- walk (between two markers);
- relay (using hockey sticks to guide a small ball 360 degrees around a series of bases);
- lie down (with eyes closed).

The class was divided into six groups, and each group performed each of the actions for one minute, with a minute's rest and changeover time. Each group was given a *hand-held tape recorder*. At the end of each action, the group recorded how their bodies felt during the exercise.

One pupil (who was unwell) used a *stopwatch* to record one-minute intervals.

After the physical education lesson, each group worked on the class *personal computer* and *word processor* to type the words they collected, which were printed in large font and presented as part of a class display on 'Our bodies in action'.

Case study 2: Key Stage 3 (Year 8)

Learning objective/National Curriculum reference

'To create and perform fluent sequences on the floor and apparatus.'

Summary of lesson content

This lesson was part of a scheme in which pupils worked on linking a series of basic actions into sequences, on the floor and on apparatus. In previous sessions, pairs had devised simple keys, where a symbol represented an action or linking movement, as a way of recording their developing sequences. They used a simple *drawing package* on a *personal computer* to create the symbols, and *printed* off the sequences in preparation for this lesson. As the sequences progressed, they were updated on the *PC*.

The teacher wished to stress the importance of smooth and fluent linking actions, so began the lesson with some short clips of *video-recorded* high-level gymnastics. The point, she stressed, was not to copy the actions, but to see how the gymnasts moved between actions smoothly and fluently. As the class watched the clip, the teacher asked pupils to identify the type of actions and links used. Through questioning, she drew from the class the key points about good linking actions. These were displayed on the whiteboard.

Once the practical part of the lesson was under way, the pupils worked in pairs on their sequences, each one of the pair offering evaluation and feedback on the other's performance. A *digital camcorder* was available for groups to record and analyse their performance. Using the instant playback, slow motion and freeze-frame facilities on the camera, pupils could see for themselves their sequences, and discuss with their partners ways to improve the quality of the movements.

These examples are not presented as models of 'perfect' practice, but rather as interesting uses of ICT, utilizing equipment readily available in most schools. It should be clear that the uses of ICT within these lessons arose out of a genuine need, and were not artificially added on. It should also be apparent that the use of ICT in these cases contributed to pupils' learning and understanding in physical education, and that many of the benefits gained would not have been available without the use of ICT.

The case studies demonstrate only a small proportion of the potential uses of ICT in physical education lessons. The list of applications presented earlier in this chapter indicates that options for the teacher are virtually endless.

Task 9.2

- Compile a list of the relevant ICT resources available to you. Include in your list CD ROMs and other software, specialist PE and sports studies equipment, audio-visual equipment and resources stored by other relevant subject areas (such as biology, sociology and psychology).
- Consult the person responsible for the school library, the ICT co-ordinator and your colleagues in PE.
- If a list like this does not already exist for PE, discuss offering your list for future use by the PE department.

Promoting learning in physical education through ICT

It should be apparent that ICT opens up new opportunities for learning and understanding, and acts as an aid in collecting, managing and manipulating information in various forms. This section offers a simple framework for considering these different functions, specifically within the context of physical education lessons.

ICT can be used in physical education to:

- gather information;
- provide stimuli for movement;
- plan and develop movement ideas;
- collect and analyse information;
- evaluate performance;
- exchange ideas with others.

These uses are considered in a little more detail below.

Gathering information

Gardner and Walsh (2000) invented the word 'worldmindedness' in recognition of one formidable aspect of ICT: the potential for technology to enable world-wide communications and information sharing. This technology has the potential to break down the physical and cultural barriers that currently separate the peoples of the world, and to make available vast stores of information that were previously inaccessible. The *Internet* and *World Wide Web* have revolutionized the way in which we can access information. In fact, the sheer quantity of information available and the ease with which it can be accessed mean that teachers need to utilize this resource with care. But, with selective use, ICT opens up whole new areas of learning for pupils in physical education.

Chapter 1 discussed the concept of physical education as, in part, *education about movement*, in which pupils come to understand the range and importance of purposeful physical activities. ICT can make a valuable contribution to this aspect of the curriculum. The next box lists a sample of the sites that are of relevance to teachers of physical education (see also Hall and Leigh, 2000; http://www.aahperd. org/; and http://pecentral.org/ for other useful Web sites).

The use of the World Wide Web in physical education lessons reflects what Kemmis, Atkin and Wright (1977) called the 'revelatory paradigm': it involves guiding pupils through a process of learning by discovery. There are other resources that can support learning of this sort, such as *videos* and *CD ROMs*. Both can provide useful sources of information for pupils in support of their study, although CD ROMs are becoming increasingly powerful, as sources of information, owing to their flexibility of use and the potential for interactive use by pupils. There are now a number of well-designed packages that are of relevance to the physical education curriculum, such as Tacklesport (www.tacklesport.com), which is a series of animated drills for a variety of sports on CD ROM, and The Ultimate Human Body (from Dorling Kindersley), which offers clear views of different aspects of the human body in action and at rest.

Useful Web sites for physical education

General PE and sport

American Alliance for Health, Physical Education, Recreation and Dance: http://www.aahperd.org/
British Sports Network: http://www.britsport.com/
Cybertown Campus – Health and Physical Education Building: http://cybertown.com/campheal.html

PE Central: http://pecentral.org/
Physical Education Association of the United Kingdom: http://www.pea.uk.com/
Sport England: http://www.english.sports.gov.uk/about/about_1.htm
Sportscore: http://www.learnfree.co.uk/sportscore
Sports Huddle: http://www.sportshuddle.com/
Sports Media: http://www.sports-media.org/
Youth Sport Trust: http://www.youthsport.net/

History and geography of sport

British Gymnastics History Milestones:
http://www.baga.co.uk/Intro.intro.htm#History
Contemporary Dance: http://www.isadoraduncan.org/
English Cricket: http://www.ecb.co.uk/
Greek Civilization – Sport: http://www.greekciv.pdx.edu/sport/sport.htm
Olympic Museum: http://www.museum.olympic.org/
Soccer (Association Football): http://www.innotts.co.uk/ÿ soccer/hist1.htm

Health and exercise

Active for Life: http://www.active.org.uk/Nrgize; http://www.nrgize.co.uk
Atlas of the Human Body: http://www.ama-assn.org/insight/gen_hlth/atlas/atlas.htm
BBC Health: http://bbc.co.uk/health/
British Heart Foundation: http://www.nhf.org.uk
Heart Rate Zone: http://www.home.connecticut.com/eoinf/heartrate.html
Wired for Health: http://www.wiredforhealth.gov.uk/

Specific sports and activities

Coach Scope (swimming): http://www.coachscope.com
CricInfo (cricket): http://www-uk.cricket.org/
Danceservice UK: http://danceservice.co.uk
International Amateur Athletics Federation: http://www.iaaf.org/TheSport/index.asp
International Rugby Board – Play the Game: http://www.irfb.com/playgame.htm
Netball Resource Page: http://www.ucl.ac.uk/uczcw11/netball.htm
TennisOrg UK: http://www.tennis.org.uk/

Providing stimuli for movement

Physical education teachers have always used *taped music, video, television* and *radio* as stimuli for movement. Perhaps the most obvious use has been music for dance, and teachers of this activity area are well advised to build up a varied collection of music and other types of sounds. Visual images can also inspire or guide movements, and they provide variation in the teacher's presentation of a lesson. In this regard, CD ROMs can also be useful. Other forms of audio-visual aid that may be of use to teachers include *whiteboards, models* (skeletons, organs, movable artistic models) and *slides.*

Planning and developing movement ideas

Pupil planning in physical education is usually inextricably linked to performance and evaluation. However, there may be times when it is valuable to plan and develop ideas away from the gym. This may be particularly useful in the primary phase, when greater flexibility in planning allows the teacher to combine certain aspects of the curriculum, such as English and physical education. Martyn (1999) argues that ICT, such as the use of *word processing*, offers the opportunity to allow pupils to experience the thought-enhancing effects of written language. Planning can also be facilitated through the use of *drawing packages* and *concept keyboards*, with which pupils can plan and develop apparatus layouts, gymnastics sequences, dance routines or outdoor activity checklists.

Collecting and analysing information

Making sense of information is an important aspect of learning in all Key Stages, especially from Key Stage 2 and beyond. There are numerous times when data are generated and gathered as natural parts of physical education lessons:

- scores;
- heart rates;
- fitness tests;
- times for completion of events.

Databases and *spreadsheets* allow pupils to cut down the tiresome task of representing data, and make it possible to order, analyse, see patterns and make comparisons between different aspects of the collected data. Other, more specialist, equipment can support the gathering of information. *Heart-rate monitors, digital blood-pressure analysers, stopwatches* and *other timing devices* are normally available in schools; they provide useful, specific information, reflect authentic use in exercise and sports sciences, and can be highly motivating to pupils using them.

Evaluating performance

Teachers of physical education have often used *video cameras* in their work, and they have become a standard tool at GCSE and A level (Conway, 2000). The advent of relatively cheap, hand-held *digital cameras* opens up new possibilities for pupils of all ages. As has been discussed elsewhere, feedback is an essential feature of effective teaching and learning in physical education, and the possibility of viewing and commenting upon their recent performances can be very valuable, as it is the pupils themselves who are evaluating their performance, not just the teacher or peers. In this way, pupils develop their skills of analysis from an early age, and become more receptive to the comments from others (Beashel and Sibson, 2000). Aspects of physical education that lend themselves to evaluation in this way include:

- gymnastics compositions;
- dance composition;
- team play – awareness of space and positioning;
- technique development.

Communicating ideas with others

Developments in communications technology have opened up exciting new opportunities for pupils to access information and converse with people far beyond their immediate environment. Through *Web sites* and the use of *e-mail*, pupils can engage in meaningful conversations with pupils living on the other side of the world. Teachers can arrange partnerships between schools in this country and overseas, through meeting points like SCHOOLSNET, or via links from physical education Web sites. E-mail discussions can facilitate rapid exchange of information about local sports, educational experiences and lifestyle. Pupils can also join Web-based discussion groups, and share ideas on topics being studied in schools around the world, or ask questions of 'experts', via specialist homepages. Physical education and after-school sports provision present meaningful contexts for the creation of a school's *PE homepage*, providing information on things like the calendar of sporting events, awards and results. There is even the growing possibility of face-to-face meetings with peers around the world through the introduction of *videoconferencing* facilities in some schools.

Planning and class management with ICT in physical education

ICT can be a useful addition to the teacher's repertoire of skills. However, it should be seen as a support for good teaching, not a replacement. Like any teaching strategy, ICT should be used when it can make a contribution to pupils' learning, and should be part of the more general planning and teaching approach adopted by the teacher.

Ten principles of good practice in using ICT in physical education, *10 golden rules*, are listed below:

1. Decisions regarding the use of ICT in lessons should be related directly to the objectives of the lesson.
2. The teacher should be selective in the use of resources.
3. Make sure pupils know how to use the technology and have the necessary key skills before letting them loose on it.
4. Resources should be thoroughly checked, and the teacher should make sure that he or she can operate all equipment, before the lesson.
5. Resources should be set up and ready to operate before pupils start the lesson.
6. Consider the organization of the use of ICT. Will pupils work alone, in pairs or in groups? Will they decide or will the teacher decide when ICT is required? Will pupils, teacher or another person operate and control the equipment?
7. The teacher should check pupils' understanding and on-task behaviour, as in any other aspects of the lesson.
8. Give pupils enough time to use the equipment safely, and to reflect upon their thinking and learning.
9. Try to offer regular experience of ICT, to reinforce knowledge and understanding of the technology and its use.
10. Do not feel compelled to use ICT in every instance in physical education. It is only a part of the range of options available to the teacher, and should be selected when it meets a need.

Summary

This chapter has explored the different ways in which ICT can contribute to teaching and learning in physical education. It has been suggested that it offers an exciting opportunity to motivate and support learning, but that it should not be used uncritically. The criterion for deciding to use ICT should always be whether it can contribute to the achievement of the lesson's learning objectives. Key principles of the use of ICT in physical education lessons include the following:

- The main criterion for the use of ICT in physical education lessons is its contribution to teaching and learning.
- Physical education lessons contain numerous opportunities to include interesting and challenging uses of technology.
- The use of ICT in physical education is a statutory requirement at Key Stages 3 and 4, and is good practice at Key Stages 1 and 2.

Further reading

Hall, A and Leigh, J (2000) *Using the Internet: Physical education*, Pearson, Cambridge
Hall, A and Leigh, J (2001) *ICT in PE: Policy and practice*, Pearson, Cambridge

A useful contact for videos, CD ROMs and other specialist ICT resources for physical education is Coachwise, 114 Cardigan Road, Headingley, Leeds LS6 3BJ, UK.

Specialist journals like the *British Journal of Teaching Physical Education* and the *Bulletin of Physical Education* also provide reviews of the latest ICT software for physical education. Their contact details are in the Appendix.

10 Citizenship and values education

Introduction

Views of the relationship between physical education and what can broadly be termed citizenship education have been passionate and frequently opposing. The debate, which can be traced back to the very beginnings of educational philosophy, cuts to the heart of the subject. On the one side are those for whom organized physical activities represent ideal opportunities for young people to learn of success and failure, of overcoming obstacles, of restraining one's own selfish desires for the good of the team. On the other are those who complain that a great deal of the content of physical education enshrines a competitive, antagonistic structure in which players attempt to defeat and show their superiority over others, values that it is no longer appropriate to instil in our young. The chapter examines the contribution that physical education can make to the values and citizenship agenda.

Objectives

By the end of this chapter you should:

- understand some historical aspects of the values and citizenship debate in physical education;
- be familiar with recent guidance on citizenship education;
- be familiar with some approaches to delivering values and citizenship education through physical education.

The citizenship agenda

Questions of values and education are not merely of historical or philosophical interest. Recent policy and guidance documents (for example, SCAA, 1996; QCA/DfEE, 1998; DfEE, 1999a; DfEE, 1999b) reiterate something that is self-evident for most teachers: formal education, and each of its constituent elements, should contribute systematically to all aspects of pupils' development, not least to their social and moral development, for their immediate value and for their value in preparing pupils to become active, capable and responsible members of society. Citizenship education relates closely to concepts like values education, character education, and personal, social and moral education. Each aspect has a different focus, but they all share an agenda that stresses the importance of promoting pupils' values and pupils' ability to live as informed, active members of society (see Bailey, 2000c).

An important contribution to the debate, and the main influence behind the recently introduced National Curriculum for citizenship, was the Crick Report (QCA/DfEE, 1998). The report made a case for a citizenship curriculum for all Key Stages. It identified three key dimensions: participation in democracy; the responsibilities and rights of citizens; and the value of community activity. It also developed a framework for citizenship education.

Framework for citizenship education

Guiding principles

- breadth and balance;
- coherence;
- continuity and progression;
- relevance;
- quality;
- access and inclusion.

Factors affecting the learning process

- whole-school approaches;
- teaching and learning opportunities;
- special educational needs.

Teacher assessment of learning components

- aims and purpose;
- strands;
- social and moral responsibility;
- community involvement;
- political literacy;
- essential elements;
- concepts;
- values and dispositions;
- skills and aptitudes;
- knowledge and understanding;
- social;
- moral;
- political;
- economic;
- environmental.

(QCA/DfEE, 1998: 35–46)

This framework has been broadly accepted by policy makers, and forms the basis of the Programmes of Study for citizenship. One significant change, however, is that the entitlement in this area remains *non-statutory at Key Stages 1 and 2*, and only statutory at Key Stages 3 and 4 (from 2002). The Programmes of Study identify the knowledge, skills and understanding in which pupils are expected to make progress:

- becoming informed citizens;
- developing skills of enquiry and communication;
- developing skills of participation and responsible action.

All subjects must show how they can play a role in this new agenda. Physical education seems particularly well placed to contribute to the citizenship agenda: 'it is the rationale of "character-building", of moral development, of citizenship development, of social development, that justifies the existence of physical education and athletics in educational institutions' (Stevenson, 1975: 287).

The Programmes of Study are summarized in the box below.

> ## Citizenship in the National Curriculum
>
> ### Citizenship at Key Stage 3
>
> During Key Stage 3 pupils study, reflect upon and discuss topical political, spiritual, moral, social and cultural issues, problems and events. They learn to identify the role of the legal, political, religious, social and economic institutions and systems that influence their lives and communities. They continue to be actively involved in the life of their school, neighbourhood and wider communities and learn to become more effective in public life. They learn about fairness, social justice, respect for democracy and diversity at school, local, national and global level, and through taking part responsibly in community activities.
>
> ### Citizenship at Key Stage 4
>
> During Key Stage 4 pupils continue to study, think about and discuss topical political, spiritual, moral, social and cultural issues, problems and events. They study the legal, political, religious, social, constitutional and economic systems that influence their lives and communities, looking more closely at how they work and their effects. They continue to be actively involved in the life of their school, neighbourhood and wider communities, taking greater responsibility. They develop a range of skills to help them do this, with a growing emphasis on critical awareness and evaluation. They develop knowledge, skills and understanding in these areas through, for example, learning more about fairness, social justice, respect for democracy and diversity at school, local, national and global level, and through taking part in community activities. (http://www.nc.uk.net/servlets/NCFrame?subject=PE)

Physical education as values education

The view that participation in physical activities can contribute to young people's developing values and 'characters' has a long and distinguished history. Plato warned of the consequences of an education that overemphasizes the academic at the expense of the physical. He suggested that a balance is needed, 'to produce a mind that is civilised and brave, as opposed to cowardly and uncivilised' (Lee, 1955: 145). Similar sentiments were expressed by Jean-Jacques Rousseau (Foxley, 1974) and many other educational writers, leading to the so-called 'muscular

Christianity' of 19th-century Britain, whose philosophy is summarized by the 1864 Royal Commission on Public Schools: 'The cricket and football fields... are not merely places of exercise or amusement; they help to form some of the most valuable social qualities and manly virtues...' (cited in MacIntosh, 1957: 178).

This 'cult of athleticism' (Mangan, 1981) had as its stated aim the production of individuals exemplifying the virtues felt useful to an expanding Empire: bravery, self-confidence, discrimination and so on. The emphasis was upon team sports, which were frequently organized, managed and officiated by the pupils. Learning to lead on the playing field would translate, it was hoped, to leadership in industry, business, government and the military. This faith in team sports survived until after World War I, during which generals still felt that soldiers would develop manliness, discipline, courage, loyalty and a capacity for self-sacrifice through team sports (Shields and Bredemeier, 1995).

More recently, a number of writers have sought to present physical activities, especially sporting activities, as inherently moral enterprises. Arnold (1979) is representative of a view that physical education and organized games are not simply a useful medium for values education, but rather that they are fundamentally *about* values education. Since 'sport is inherently concerned with the moral' (1979: 280), participation in such activities offers players the opportunity to practise moral virtue. Arnold interprets sport as essentially concerned with fairness. Sport is fair because players willingly follow the rules even when there may be an advantage for them in not doing so. The source of fairness in sport, therefore, does not lie with the referee, but with the players and their motivation to conduct themselves in appropriate ways. Another advocate, Aspin (1975: 49–50), has similarly argued that: 'It is possible for one to treat the whole topic of sport, not as means to promote the ends of moral education, but as being, in certain respects, activities necessarily underpinned by and shot through with presuppositions that are of an irreducibly ethical character... They may therefore, to some extent, be regarded as moral enterprises.'

The teacher is, thus, presented with a marvellously accessible model of values education: 'simply by seriously engaging pupils in competitive games and athletics, a teacher is of necessity implicitly pursuing aims that embody moral values, for such values are enshrined in many of the rules which constitute these activities' (Meakin, 1982: 68).

Recent governments have endorsed this position. In the report, *Sport: Raising the Game* (DNH, 1995: 2), the then prime minister, John Major, enthused:

> Competitive sport teaches valuable lessons which last for life. Every game delivers both a winner and loser. Sportsmen must learn to be both. Sport only thrives if both parties play by the rules, and accept the results with good grace. It is one of the best means of learning how to live alongside and make a contribution as part of a team.

Before we are carried away with such enthusiasm, it is worth sounding a note of caution. It is unlikely that those who follow the exploits of some of our most talented sports players will be easily convinced that participation *necessarily* enshrines moral values: intimidation of officials and aggression towards other players routinely take place in professional football; temper tantrums of elite tennis players are as memorable as their exquisite stroke play; corruption in boxing is now taken for granted. In light of modern sport, Arnold and Aspin's claims sound a little naive. How can sport enshrine values when so many of our sporting greats are clearly morally vacuous?

Of course, defenders of the view of sport as a moral enterprise would probably agree with this description of some professional sports players. It is not elite sport that is being defended, they might claim, but the recreational sport of the majority, and the sport and physical activities that take place in schools. They are hardly the same things. The problem caused by using one word to describe a range of events from an infant's playground game to the World Cup interferes with a clear and fair judgement of the evidence. It has been suggested that we distinguish sport (concerned with participation, pleasure and friendship) and athletics (contesting for a prize). In other words, there is an essential difference between the physical activities that most people practise for pleasure and those that provide employment for an elite few. A distinction is necessary because the two types of activities have entirely different aims and outcomes.

Task 10.1

Do you agree with the distinction between sport and athletics? What values underpin each category?

Arnold (1979: 278) has claimed that the following of rules in sport is inextricably linked to the possession and development of values and 'character'. But surely this misinterprets the function of rules in sport, which simply serve to make the activity possible. They need have nothing to do with the moral conduct of the players. For example, driving a car requires adherence to the rules of the road, but there is no reason why it has to be understood as a moral activity, nor why driving should be understood as a 'vehicle' for values education. In fact, it is quite conceivable that rules could be devised that specifically encourage injury or cruelty (which may be the case with unlicensed boxing and fox hunting). It would be ridiculous to suggest that these activities would count as moral enterprises, and that participants would receive a values education simply by sticking to the rules.

It is quite possible for people to play a game fairly (in that they follow the rules), and have no moral regard for their opponents. In discussions of values education in physical education, therefore, it is vital to consider questions of feelings and affection, and the development of particular attitudes, such as caring, tolerance, benevolence, loyalty, sympathy and compassion (Wright, 1987). Since these qualities need not necessarily arise during physical education lessons, they must be the result of something more than the activities themselves. In order to understand what this additional factor might be, it is useful briefly to review the empirical data related to physical education and sport, and social and values development.

The most comprehensive review of the literature on this subject is by David Shields and Brenda Bredemeier (1995). Their conclusion is that the research evidence neither supports nor falsifies the claim that participation in physical activities develops appropriate values and behaviour traits. In fact, a more accurate summary would be that *some* studies suggest that participation can contribute to values and social development, and *others* suggest that it cannot (or worse, that it can actually be damaging). For example, many parents and teachers feel that organized physical activities encourage co-operation in children, but some studies found an increase in hostility to others and a decrease in generosity and altruism in some pupils. Likewise, it is well established that sports players are less likely than non-participants to engage in delinquent behaviour; however, some studies have found that regular players show less sporting attitudes and values than others do.

The evidence seems to show that sport and physical activities can have either a positive or a negative effect on children's attitudes and behaviours. One possible explanation for this apparent anomaly is that researchers have usually focused on the activities in which children participated, rather than the way those activities were presented. Most of the empirical studies carried out in this area assume that learning outcomes in physical education are solely derived from the activity being taught. This is not the case. The way that the activity is taught is at least as important. This distinction between the *content* and the *context* of physical education lessons is of fundamental importance for the present discussion: values education will not happen by itself, simply as a result of the teacher organizing a game and enforcing the rules.

Content and context in physical education

Almond (2000: 6–7) offers a useful distinction between educational values that focus on the content of lessons and those that emphasize opportunities for interpersonal competencies, for friendships and community. Of course, these values should not be considered independently. Rather, they are closely linked: teachers ought to plan with both content and context in mind. Just as teachers would aim to offer opportunities for progression in the physical skills and techniques that are taught in physical education classes, so they should strive to develop pupils' social skills.

In planning for education in values and for citizenship, it is important that teachers do not conceive of their task in too technical a way: it is not simply a matter of training pupils into certain forms of behaviour. Perhaps most would agree with Wright (1992: 124) that education should aim to nurture certain qualities widely deemed to be desirable and necessary for the continuation of a democratic society: 'self-confidence leavened by an agreeable humility, curiosity, courage, persistence, kindness, gentleness, a care for the less fortunate, and a care for other forms of life'.

However, it would be a mistake to move from an agreement that these might be necessary elements of an adequate values education to the assumption that they are enough. Ethical living requires something more than simply following a set of principles that can be memorized and applied like an equation. Frequently, decisions have to be made between different kinds of good: between truth and loyalty, self and others, short- and long-term benefit (Kidder, 1995). The recognition of this fact does not remove the need to establish and distil the principles upon which civilized society is based, but it does stress the importance of supporting such values education with reflection on the conflicting pressures and painful choices (sometimes between two rights) that are bound to confront each of us, at different times in our lives:

> The important point for learning morality and citizenship is to understand that making moral decisions is as much about making hard choices, and having the intellectual and emotional equipment to make them properly, as it is about knowing the rules of moral conduct. We can learn ground rules, and principles which we should try to follow, but there will always be cases in which the moral response is not automatic or obvious – cases where we are caught between conflicting principles, cases where diagnosis of the problem and practical interpretation of an abstract principle are difficult.
> (Bentley, 1998: 62)

There is some evidence that physical education can provide a worthwhile environment for the sort of values education outlined above. One approach that has been found to be effective is called 'built-in dilemmas/dialogue' (BIDD) (Romance, Weiss and Bockoven, 1986), which is summarized in Task 10.2 below. In the BIDD approach, pupils are routinely confronted by moral dilemmas arising during physical education lessons.

Task 10.2

Built-in dilemmas/dialogue strategies:

1. Ask the pupils if the activity in which they have just taken part was fair. Did everybody take part? Did they all have fun? How do they decide what makes a game fair? Discuss issues such as being sporting, co-operation and trust as they arise in lessons.
2. Plan tasks with built-in problems or omissions, and encourage pupils to change the rules as they wish.
3. Play games with and without a referee, and discuss the advantages and disadvantages of each.

Another, widely cited example of values education is the 'Responsibility Model' (Hellison and Templin, 1991). The focus of this approach is the promotion of pupils' sense of responsibility. Hellison hypothesized a series of levels and sub-levels, each reflecting goals towards which individuals aim to progress. There is no intention that these levels represent developmental stages through which pupils move (although they can be interpreted in this way). Rather, they articulate the kinds of responsibilities that pupils need to consider in everyday contexts:

This educational process is intended to cause students to *feel* empowered and purposeful, to experience making responsible commitments to themselves and others, to strive to develop themselves despite external forces, to be willing to risk popularity to live by a set of principles, to understand their essential relatedness to others, and to distinguish between their own personal preferences and activities that impinge on their rights and welfare of others.

(Hellison and Templin, 1991: 104)

Accordingly, these goals are shared and discussed with pupils, to offer a common vocabulary for the teacher and pupils. Likewise, certain strategies are suggested that can help pupils become more aware of, experience, make decisions about and reflect upon their goals: 'This model requires a conceptualisation of the teaching act that is different from more traditional models. If students are to become responsible, they must experience some responsibility' (Hellison and Templin, 1991: 108). The model is summarized in the box below.

The Responsibility Model

Levels

- Level 1 – self-control and respect for the rights and feelings of others:
  - self-control;
  - inclusion;
  - negotiating conflicts;
  - internalizing respect.
- Level 2 – participation and effort:
  - going through the motions;
  - exploring effort;
  - redefining success.
- Level 3 – self-direction:
  - independence;
  - goal setting;
  - knowledge base;
  - planning and evaluating.
- Level 4 – caring and helping:
  - supporting others;
  - helping others;
  - group welfare.

Strategies

- awareness;
- experience;
- choice;
- problem solving/student sharing;
- self-reflection;
- counselling time;
- teaching qualities.

The virtue of this approach is that it offers a degree of progression and structure. A weakness, however, is that it seems rather individualistic and too narrowly focused upon the behaviour of individual pupils. The emphasis throughout is *self*-responsibility, and there is an absence of the development of a sense of *social* responsibility and community that is emphasized in the National Curriculum citizenship requirements. This suggests an extension of the model.

Physical education and a sense of community

Bentley (1998) draws upon child psychology to construct a model of values and citizenship education in which the child's awareness grows from the self outwards (Figure 10.1).

Like the Responsibility Model, this model offers a clear and simple model of children's developing sense of responsibility. However, here the child is explicitly located within the wider contexts of community and society. The Responsibility Model generally operates at the level of 'self', progressing only at the last stage to 'relationships'. In order for it to address adequately issues of community and society, perhaps an extension is required. This is offered by Bailey (2000c).

Figure 10.1   A child's growing awareness of values and society (based on Bentley, 1998)

A 'Social Responsibility Model' (Bailey, 2000c)

- Level 5 – community:
  - co-operation;
  - mutual assistance;
  - civic responsibility;
  - citizenship.

Strategies

- co-operative tasks and challenges;
- discussion/debate;
- community projects;
- voluntary work.

The idea of 'social responsibility' lies at the heart of the National Curriculum for citizenship. This is evident in the selection of the three aspects of citizenship in which pupils are said to make progress:

- becoming informed citizens;
- developing skills of enquiry and communication;
- developing skills of participation and responsible action.

These themes form the basis of the learning outcomes that are identified at each Key Stage, and indicate the sorts of skills and aptitudes, knowledge and understanding that pupils should acquire as they progress through school.

Bentley (1998) outlined criteria for successful implementation of citizenship education:

- Issues should matter to pupils.
- They should be rooted in the local environment and be encountered every day.
- They should be active and practical.

Since physical activities are of central importance in the lives of many children, they form ideal media for discussing questions of citizenship and values in a context that is meaningful and important to children. Issues of morality, community and politics move from abstraction in classroom discussions to meaningful and significant questions of the day in the context of physical activities.

Tables 10.1 and 10.2 suggest some ways in which the physical education curriculum can be utilized in support of citizenship education. The examples given

Table 10.1 Citizenship curriculum at Key Stage 3 with physical education links

Pupils Should Be Taught:	*Example Physical Education Links*
to justify orally and in writing a personal opinion about political, spiritual, moral, social and cultural issues, problems and events	Discuss: cheating and drug-enhanced performance in athletics; racism in sport; ability and disability; nationalism and the Olympic Games; whether there are boys' and girls' games.
to negotiate, decide and take part responsibly in both school and community-based activities	Take part in problem-solving activities in an outdoor setting; games making; life-saving challenges. Help organize after-school sports clubs.
to use their imagination to consider other people's experiences and be able to think about, express and explain views that are not their own	Compose, perform and appreciate dances exploring different perspectives on bullying; cultures/religions different from their own, etc.
about the importance of resolving conflict fairly	Take part in built-in dilemmas/dialogue activities (see text).
the significance of the media in society	Research different ways that particular groups of sports players (women, disabled, ethnic minorities etc) are represented in different media.

Table 10.2   Including citizenship in Key Stage 1 physical education

Knowledge and Understanding	*Example Physical Education Links*
By the end of Key Stage 1, pupils should be able to:	
recognize how the concept of fairness can be applied in a reasoned and reflective way to aspects of their personal and social life	Play a simple game in which the rules have not been fully worked out. What other rules are needed to play the game fairly? Why is it important for games to be fair?
understand the different kinds of responsibility that they take on, in helping others, respecting differences or looking after shared property	Give co-operation and privacy in changing for PE. Help set up gymnastic apparatus. Assist partner in dance composition. Practise skill activities with a partner and offer simple suggestions for improvement.
know about the nature and basis of the rules in the classroom, at school and at home; also, whenever possible, know how to frame rules themselves; understand that different rules can apply in different contexts and can serve different purposes	Pupils devise a set of simple safety rules for gymnastics lessons. How are these rules different from class/school rules on behaviour? Why do we need rules in games? Adapt the rules of a small-sided game. How can we make sure everybody has fun? How can we encourage every player to join in?
understand the language used to describe feelings associated with aspects of relationships with others	Pupils compose, perform and evaluate a short dance-drama on the theme of friends. Discuss issues arising from partner or group work.
know about the different kinds of relationships that exist between pupils and between adults and pupils; also have some notion that the power in such relationships can be exercised responsibly and fairly or irresponsibly and unfairly	Small groups play a simple game in which they take turns acting as referee or scorer. Discuss the role of referees and scorers. Why are they important? How can they be unfair?

relate to Key Stages 3 and 1 (the former takes as a starting point National Curriculum guidance, whilst the latter draws on the phrases from the Crick Report, as there are currently no National Curriculum Programmes of Study at Key Stages 1 and 2).

Summary

This chapter has attempted to articulate the contribution that physical education can make to the areas of citizenship and values education. The teachers' role in planning in this area is of fundamental importance, and cannot be overstated. Once the importance of explicit and systematic planning is acknowledged, physical education activities stand out as ideal media for citizenship and values education.

Key issues to consider include:

- Physical activities hold an unequalled place in children's values, and offer distinctive opportunities to contribute to citizenship and values education.
- Context, as well as content, of physical education needs to be considered in planning.
- How teachers present activities and the values they reflect is at least as important as the tasks carried out by pupils.

Since these activities are held in high regard and can often take place outside the school day, when conceived of appropriately in terms of both content and context, they provide the medium for lifelong values and citizenship education.

Further reading

Bailey, R P (2000) *Teaching Values and Citizenship Across the Curriculum*, Kogan Page, London

Hellison, D R and Templin, T J (1991) *A Reflective Approach to Teaching Physical Education*, Human Kinetics, Champaign, IL

Shields, D L and Bredemeier, B J (1995) *Character Development and Physical Education*, Human Kinetics, Champaign, IL

11 Meeting the new class

Introduction

This brief chapter will discuss important issues associated with a teacher's first encounters with a class. Much of the subject matter will reiterate points raised elsewhere in this book. Nevertheless, first impressions last, and it is worth giving a little thought to the ways in which teachers can create the most appropriate impression in their earliest meetings with pupils. Wragg and Wood (1984a) state the situation bluntly: 'The success or failure of a whole year may rest on the impression created, the ethos, the rules and relationships established during the first two or three weeks in September.'

Objectives

By the end of this chapter you should:

- understand the importance of early meetings with a class;
- know how to plan effectively and appropriately for these early meetings.

There is widespread agreement among experienced teachers that attention and effort are required at the early stages of the teacher–pupil relationship to establish appropriate working climates for the rest of the year. It is also recognized that trainee teachers are presented with particular difficulties in this regard since they often join a class after expectations, routines and relationships have been developed and established.

Many trainee and newly qualified physical education teachers admit that meeting new classes for the first time is one of their main areas of concern (Mawer,

1995). By the nature of the concern, these feelings of nervousness and uncertainty are usually short-lived, and most teachers feel considerably more at ease once the first few weeks are out of the way. It is important to recognize, however, that these early encounters between teachers and pupils are of great significance for subsequent teaching and learning.

First impressions last, and it is worth while for the teacher to make the most of these impressions. What happens during a teacher's first meetings with a class is likely to establish the kind of relationship that he or she will have to work with for the rest of the year. In their study of first encounters of experienced and inexperienced teachers in secondary schools, Wragg and Wood (1984a) revealed a substantial combined effort by experienced teachers at the start of the year. In another study, Evertson and Emmer (1982) found great differences between more and less effective teachers in behaviour at the start of the school year. Wragg and Wood (1984a: 77) found that experienced teachers had very clear ideas of what they were going to do in terms of class management strategies *before* the year had begun:

> Most sought to establish some kind of dominant presence... tempered any initial harshness with humour, and conveyed to their class that they were in charge, using their eyes, movement and gesture to enhance that they were trying to do. There was a strong moral dimension to some of the classroom rules, and they strove to establish these substantially in the very first lesson.

The same study found that inexperienced and ineffective teachers tended to be less clear about their expectations during these early encounters. Some said that they would establish rules and procedures as the need arose. There is a consensus that this is not best practice. Rules, routine and expectations should be thoroughly thought out in advance, and their introduction and reinforcement should be planned explicitly into early lessons.

The principles emphasized during this chapter should be understood to apply well beyond the first lesson. Early meetings are often characterized by pupils and teachers sizing each other up. It is during later lessons, perhaps the second or third meeting, that some pupils begin to test the teacher and the boundaries within which they will be allowed to operate. New teachers find that it is during these subsequent meetings that bolder pupils start to challenge their authority with minor acts of misbehaviour, and it is then that many of the matters discussed here come into full effect.

If the teacher does not establish that he or she is in control during these early encounters, there is a serious risk of the pupils concluding that they are. Many teachers compare their early meetings with new classes to 'battles' that they must win, as otherwise the children will take control and the teacher will become demoralized.

Manner and relationships

'Whether you are aware of it or not, you will establish an ethos within a short space of time, so it is desirable that you create one that is favourable and to your advantage' (Cohen, Manion and Morrison, 1996: 192).

Effective teachers present a firm, confident image during these early meetings. This need not have a cold or unwelcoming character, but should make it clear to the pupils that the teacher expects them to comply with expectations and standards of behaviour. Mawer (1995), for example, cites a number of experienced physical educators who suggest that a teacher's manner during early encounters should be confident, assertive, yet also approachable. One head of department offered the following guidance: 'Don't try to be their big friend – it doesn't pay. They must know where the line is drawn.' And an advisory teacher suggested: 'Assert yourself in the class – be approachable but not overfamiliar' (Mawer, 1995: 103). Many also emphasized the value of getting to know pupils, and of laying the foundations for positive relationships. Selective praise and encouragement can motivate pupils to co-operate and to adhere to expectations. Learning names early in the year eases communication and also implies that the teacher has a genuine interest in the pupils and views them as individuals.

Pupils seem to prefer teachers who are firm but fair, are consistent, stimulating, interested in individuals and have a sense of humour (Wragg and Wood, 1984b). It can be a challenge to strike a balance between firmness and warmth. If teachers go too far in the direction of firmness, there is a risk that pupils will view them as aggressive or bossy, and this will endanger the development of positive working relationships. If they go too far the other way, pupils may see them as soft or weak, and may challenge their authority. Of course, relationships are dynamic and change over time. It is in teachers' best interests to regulate this change. A reasonable approach is to begin the year from a position of control and dominance, and to gradually make concessions to pupils as the year progresses. It is much easier to do this than to regain control after pupils have acquired the upper hand.

Rules

The importance of rules, routine and expectations in physical education lessons has been discussed in some detail in Chapter 4. The establishment of such procedures begins with the very first meeting. These will be developed and extended throughout the year, but it is during the earliest encounters that pupils are first presented with standards. It is also during these initial meetings that pupils find out whether the teacher is prepared and able to enforce these rules.

The potential scope for rules is great, and can include procedures for entering the gym or hall, talking, sharing equipment or apparatus, safety and clothing. The difficulty is that it would be neither practical nor desirable to present pupils with a comprehensive list of rules and procedures during their first lesson. A better approach is to establish a set of basic rules during the first encounters with a class, and elaborate upon these as time goes on. By restricting the number of rules in this way, it is more likely that pupils will remember them, and that the teacher will be able to ensure that they are adhered to.

Categories for rules during early meetings might include the following:

- safety;
- clothing/appearance;
- talking/listening;
- movement into/around the area;
- dealing with others;
- dealing with equipment and facilities;
- attitudes towards participation.

Task 11.1

- Compile a list of basic rules with which it is appropriate to begin the year. This list should be made up of a limited number of items, and should focus upon the expectations that are most urgent or refer to matters most likely to arise early in the school year.
- Refer to Chapter 4 for possible rules or headings.
- Discuss your list with colleagues, and compare it with the rules that they enforce during the first meetings with a class.

Evertson and Emmer (1982) found that effective teachers tended to have simple, workable rules, and that they introduced and reinforced these rules in a systematic way. Sometimes, the lesson content is less important than the process of learning. Especially early in the year, it is worth devoting some time to activities that enhance pupils' abilities to work safely and sensibly in the physical education area. In fact, it is unlikely that learning will be facilitated at all without certain standards of behaviour being firmly established. Teachers spend a considerable proportion of early lessons introducing and reinforcing rules, routine and expectations. Of course, these things should not make up the total lesson time, but time invested in laying the ground rules is usually time well spent, as it saves an enormous amount of time over the coming year and contributes to pupils' abilities to regulate their own work.

Probably the most common rule enforced by teachers of any subject relates to talking when the teacher is talking. There are logistical reasons for emphasizing this from the start: if pupils do not listen to the teacher's instructions, they will not know what to do. Within the context of the first meetings, though, an even more significant reason relates to the need for pupils to recognize and adhere to the teacher's control and dominance. When attention is called for, it is an instruction not a request. So, it is important to insist upon absolute silence and not to continue speaking until this has been achieved.

Some teachers talk of 'playing the waiting game'. They wait calmly until everyone in the class displays appropriate behaviour. As they greet a group at the start of a lesson, they wait until all are looking in silence before continuing. Anger or frustration is not useful at this stage, since it shows the pupils that they can control the teacher's behaviour. A better approach is to take a prominent position whilst looking pupils in the eye (or some pupils from different parts of the group), and not proceed until all comply. There is a danger, of course, that this may take some time. After a while the class will realize that it is much easier and less boring to do as the teacher asks. However, we should all take a warning from a cartoon that appeared some years ago in a teachers' newspaper, which showed the consequences of taking this strategy too far (cited in McManus, 1994). Pupils are depicted in a state of disorder: paper aircraft and chair legs fill the air; cobwebs stretch from the teacher to the walls and ceiling. The caption reads: 'I'm still waiting'!

Planning and preparing for the first lessons

Great care and attention needs to be given to the planning and preparation of the first lessons with a class. Thorough planning is an effective way of combating nerves and anxieties; it is also something that lies within the control of the teacher.

Teachers vary in their use of information on classes they are about to teach. Many experienced teachers in Wragg and Wood's (1984a) study preferred not to find out too much about the previous behaviour and background of pupils, and tried, instead, to draw their own conclusions on individuals and groups. Less experienced teachers usually feel better prepared and more confident approaching a class about whom they have been reasonably well briefed, especially about potential behavioural problems. However, such information should always be treated with care, since it is too easy to create a self-fulfilling prophecy of pupils' behaviour: a teacher who expects certain individuals or groups to misbehave often finds that expectation realized. It is also wise to remember that pupils behave differently with different teachers and in different situations. If a pupil is troublesome during dance, it does not automatically follow that he or she will behave that way in other sessions.

There are some kinds of information about a class that every teacher needs to have. It is necessary to know about the special educational needs or medical conditions of the pupils. Do any pupils have sensory impairment, asthma or a physical disability? Do any have general movement difficulties? Are there any pupils with communication difficulties? And so on. It is also useful to have a clear appreciation of the subject matter already covered by a class, and some indication of the range of ability within the group. Finding out the sort of activities done with a class allows their next teacher to present new and challenging work, which is generally more likely to be more interesting and motivating for pupils than simply repeating activities with which they are very familiar. Of course, there are some times when it is worth while to revise and reinforce learning, and other times when it is good to plan tasks that are known to be enjoyed by a class.

As was discussed earlier in this chapter, the earliest lessons with pupils are opportunities to establish rules, routines and procedures. Lesson content, therefore, is almost of secondary importance after the need to enforce expectations of behaviour and work. The approach advocated by one head of department in Mawer's (1995: 101) study reflects the views of many: 'First of all establish ground rules for a high standard of behaviour, appearance and expectations of pupils; then concentrate on content of lessons and improving standards.'

Activities during these first lessons should not be too adventurous or complex. It is worth while to start with tasks that are relatively simple to organize, perhaps games or whole-class activities with which pupils are familiar, which they enjoy and which offer a high likelihood of success and achievement. These early lessons need to be thoroughly planned, placing an emphasis upon periods of potential difficulties, such as entering the area, getting equipment, getting into groups and transitions between tasks. The impression generated during these early encounters should be that this teacher is confident, competent and in control of the pupils and the lesson.

In secondary schools, where teachers do not bring a class to the physical education area, it is generally a sound principle for the teacher to be standing ready to receive a class before they arrive. It is essential during early meetings. To do so shows that the teacher is in control, and that he or she invites the pupils into *the teacher's area* on *the teacher's terms*. Moreover, it is much easier to enforce appropriate behaviour as pupils arrive for a lesson than to settle an already misbehaving group.

Primary teachers do not usually have the benefit of meeting their class at the hall door. Instead, they must walk them from the classroom to the physical education lesson. Nevertheless, it is certainly worth stopping for a moment outside the area and bringing the class back to order and silence before entering. In some small way, it is possible to send a message to the pupils that they are entering a special place, with its own rules and expectations.

Once in the physical education area, the lesson should begin with a short introduction and then proceed briskly to practical activities. In their study of pupils' views of teaching, Wragg and Wood (1984a) found that the vast majority expected teachers to introduce themselves with their name and some personal details about interests or hobbies.

Summary

As the old saying goes, you only get one chance to make a first impression. First meetings with a new class are valuable opportunities to lay foundations that support teaching and learning for the rest of the year and beyond. This chapter has outlined some strategies to help make the most of these early encounters. Key points include the following:

- Effective and well-planned early meetings with a class are essential in the establishment of expectations for the rest of the year.
- A limited number of rules and expectations should be presented during these early lessons.

Further reading

Mawer, M (1995) *The Effective Teaching of Physical Education*, Chapter 6, Longman, London

Robertson, J (1989) *Effective Classroom Control*, Chapter 3, Hodder and Stoughton, London

Wragg, E C (ed) (1984) *Classroom Teaching Skills*, Chapter 3, Croom Helm, London

Appendix

Five really useful books for the physical education teacher

Armstrong, N (1996) *New Directions in Physical Education: Change and innovation*, Cassell, London
Useful edited collection, including excellent chapters on special needs, giftedness, health and development.

Bailey, R P and Macfadyen, T M (eds) (2000) *Teaching Physical Education 5–11*, Continuum, London
Although written for primary teachers, this is a useful guide to teaching physical education in general. There are chapters on many topics that extend the discussions in this book, like children's movement development, curriculum leadership and practical information on each of the activity areas.

Green, K and Hardman, K (1998) *Physical Education: A reader*, Meyer and Meyer, Aachen, Germany
As the title suggests, this is a collection of articles on different aspects of physical education. Contains some classic papers, many of which have been updated in light of recent reforms.

Mawer, M (1995) *The Effective Teaching of Physical Education*, Longman, London
A very thorough review of research into effective teaching and learning in physical education. Goes into greater detail on many of the issues discussed in this book.

Rink, J E (1993) *Teaching Physical Education for Learning*, Mosby, St Louis, MO
Very clear guide from the USA. It is particularly strong on skills of task presentation and instruction.

Useful addresses and contacts

American Alliance for Health, Physical Education, Recreation and Dance
1900 Association Drive
Reston
VA 20191
USA
Tel: +1 703 476 3400
e-mail: ginfo@aahperd.org
Web site: http://www.aahperd.org/
Largest US organization in this area; publishes *Journal of Physical Education, Recreation & Dance*.

Australian Council for Health, Physical Education and Recreation
214 Port Road
(or PO Box 304)
Hindmarsh
South Australia 5007
Tel: +61 8 8340 3388
e-mail: achper@achper.org.au
Web site: http://www.achper.org.au
Publishes a number of useful journals and professional resources.

British Association of Advisers and Lecturers in Physical Education
Saltwells EDC
Bowling Green Road
Netherton
Dudley
West Midlands DY2 9LY
Tel: (01384) 813711
e-mail: info@BAALPE.org
Web site: http://www.baalpe.org
A professional association for advisers, lecturers, inspectors, consultants, advisory teachers and other professionals with qualifications in physical education, sport and dance; publishes the *Bulletin of Physical Education*.

Central Council for Physical Recreation
Francis House
Francis Street
London SW1P 1DE
Tel: (020) 7828 3163
Web site: http://ccpr.org.uk
Umbrella organization representing sport and organized physical activities.

Department of Education – Northern Ireland
Rathgael House
Bangor
Co Down BT19 7PR
e-mail: deni@nics.gov.uk
Web site: http://www.deni.gov.uk/

Department for Education and Skills (formerly Department for Education and Employment)
Sanctuary Buildings
Great Smith Street
London SW1P 3BT
Tel: (0870) 000 2288
e-mail: info@dfee.gov.uk
Web site: http://www.dfee.gov.uk/
The UK government department with overall responsibility for education, training and work.

National Assembly for Wales Training and Education Department
Training and Education Department
National Assembly for Wales
Cathays Park
Cardiff CF10 3NQ
Tel: (029) 2082 5111
e-mail: education.training@wales.gsi.gov.uk
Web site: http://www.wales.gov.uk/subieducationtraining/index.htm

National Coaching Foundation
114 Cardigan Road
Headingley
Leeds LS6 3BJ
Tel: (0113) 274 4802
e-mail: coaching@ncf.org.uk
Web site: http://www.ncf.org.uk/
Concerned with the support and training of sports coaches; its trading arm – Coachwise – is a very useful source of resources for teaching and coaching.

National Council for School Sport
95 Boxley Drive
West Bridgford
Nottingham NG2 7GN
Tel: (0115) 923 1229
e-mail: patsmith@schoolsport.freeserve.co.uk

Office for Standards in Education
Alexandra House
33 Kingsway
London WC2B 6SE
Tel: (020) 7421 6800
Web site: http://www.ofsted.gov.uk/
OFSTED's remit is to improve standards of achievement and quality of education through regular independent inspection, public reporting and informed independent advice.

Physical Education Association of Ireland
University of Limerick
National Technology Park
Limerick
Tel: +353 61 330442
e-mail: peai@ul.ie

Physical Education Association of the United Kingdom
Ling House
25 London Road
Reading
Berkshire RB1 5AQ
Tel: (01189) 316240
e-mail: enquiries@pea.uk.com
Web site: http://www.pea.uk.com
The leading representative body for physical education in the United Kingdom; publishes *British Journal of Teaching Physical Education*.

Qualifications and Curriculum Authority
83 Piccadilly
London W1J 8QA
Tel: (020) 7509 5555
Web site: http://www.qca.org.uk/
QCA offers advice and materials to promote quality and coherence in education and training.

Scottish Executive Education Department
Victoria Quay
Edinburgh EH6 6QQ
e-mail: ceu@scotland.gov.uk
Web site: http://www.scotland.gov.uk/who/dept_education.asp

Sport England
16 Upper Woburn Place
London WC1H 0QP
Tel: (020) 7273 1500
e-mail: info@english.sports.gov.uk
Web site: http://www.sportengland.org/
Sport England's objective is to lead the development of sport in England by influencing and serving the public, private and voluntary sectors; formerly the English Sports Council.

Sports Council for Northern Ireland
House of Sport
Upper Malone Road
Belfast BT9 5LA
Tel: (028) 9038 1222
Web site: www.sportni.org.uk

Sports Council for Wales
Sophia Gardens
Cardiff CF11 9SW
Tel: (029) 2030 0500
Web site: http://www.sports-council-wales.co.uk/default2.htm

Sportscotland
Caledonia House
South Gyle
Edinburgh EH12 9DQ
Tel: (0131) 317 7200
Web site: http://www.sportscotland.org.uk/

Teacher Training Agency
Portland House
Stag Place
London SW1E 5TT
Tel: (020) 7925 3700
e-mail: teaching@ttainfo.co.uk
Web site: http://www.canteach.gov.uk/
Governmental body concerned with attracting and training school teachers in the UK.

UK Sport
40 Bernard Street
London WC1N 1ST
Tel: (020) 7841 9500
e-mail: info@uksport.gov.uk
Web site: http://www.uksport.gov.uk/
Takes the lead among the home country sports councils in all aspects requiring strategic planning and administration, co-ordination or representation for the benefit of the UK as a whole.

Youth Sport Trust
Rutland Building
Loughborough University
Loughborough
Leicestershire LE11 3TU
Tel: (01509) 228293
Web site: http://www.youthsport.net/yst/
A registered charity supporting young people in sport; produces TOPS and SPORTABILITY schemes.

References

Adams, R S and Biddle, B J (1970) *The Realities of Teaching*, Holt, Rinehart and Winston, New York

Almond, L (1996) A new vision for physical education, in *New Directions in Physical Education: Change and innovation*, ed N Armstrong, Cassell, London

Almond, L (1997) *Physical Education in Schools*, Kogan Page, London

Almond, L (2000) Physical education and primary schools, in *Teaching Physical Education 5–11*, ed R P Bailey and T M Macfadyen, Continuum, London

Armstrong, N (1990) *New Directions in Physical Education*, vol 1, Human Kinetics, Champaign, IL

Armstrong, N (1992) *New Directions in Physical Education*, vol 2, Human Kinetics, Champaign, IL

Armstrong, N (1996) *New Directions in Physical Education: Change and innovation*, Cassell, London

Arnold, P J (1979) *Meaning in Movement, Sport and Physical Education*, Heinemann, London

Aspin, D (1975) Games, winning and education – some further comment, *Cambridge Journal of Education*, **5** (1), pp 51–61

BAALPE (1995) *Safe Practice in Physical Education*, BAALPE, Dudley

Bailey, R P (1999a) Play, health and physical development, in *Young Children Learning*, ed T David, Paul Chapman Publishing, London

Bailey, R P (1999b) Physical education: action, play and movement, in *The Curriculum for 7–11 Year Olds*, ed J Riley and R Prentice, Paul Chapman Publishing, London

Bailey, R P (2000a) Movement development and the primary school child, in *Teaching Physical Education 5–11*, ed R P Bailey and T M Macfadyen, Continuum, London

Bailey R P (2000b) Planning and preparation for effective teaching, in *Teaching Physical Education 5–11*, ed R P Bailey and T M Macfadyen, Continuum, London

Bailey, R P (2000c) The value and values of physical education and sport, in *Teaching Values and Citizenship Across the Curriculum: Educating children for the world*, ed R Bailey, Kogan Page, London

Bailey, R P and Macfadyen, T M (eds) (2000) *Teaching Physical Education 5–11*, Continuum, London

Bailey, R P and Robertson, C R (2000) Including *all* pupils in primary school physical education, in *Teaching Physical Education 5–11*, ed R P Bailey and T M Macfadyen, Continuum, London

Barnsford, J D, Brown, A L and Cocking, R R (1999) *How People Learn: Brain, mind, experience and school*, National Academy Press, Washington, DC

Barton, L (1993) Disability, empowerment and physical education, in *Equality, Education and Physical Education*, Falmer, London

Beashel, P and Sibson, A (2000) ICT – help or hindrance?, *British Journal of Teaching Physical Education*, **31** (2), pp 6–8

Bennett, N and Dunne, E (1994) Managing groupwork, in *Teaching and Learning in the Secondary School*, ed B Moon and A S Mayes, Routledge, London

Bentley, T (1998) *Learning Beyond the Classroom: Education for a changing world*, Routledge, London

Berry, C (1994) *Your Voice and How To Use It*, Virgin Publishing, London

Birtwistle, G and Brodie, D (1991) Children's attitudes towards physical education, *Health Education Research*, **6**, pp 465–78

Bjorkvold, J-R (1989) *The Muse Within: Creativity and communication, song and play from childhood through maturity*, HarperCollins, New York

Black, K (1999) All inclusive, *PE and Sport Today*, **1**, Winter, pp 27–29

Black, K and Haskins, D (1996) Including all children in TOP PLAY and BT TOP SPORT, *Primary PE Focus*, Winter, pp 9–11

Bott, J (1997) Developing lesson plans and units of work, in *Learning to Teach Physical Education in the Secondary School*, ed S Capel, Routledge, London

Brown, G (1975) *Microteaching*, Methuen, London

Brown, G and Armstrong, S (1984) Explaining and explanations, in *Classroom Teaching Skills*, ed E C Wragg, Croom Helm, London

Bruner, J (1983) *Child's Talk: Learning to use language*, Oxford University Press, Oxford

Bunker, D (1994) *Primary Physical Education: Implementing the National Curriculum*, Cambridge University Press, Cambridge

Capel, S (ed) (1997) *Learning to Teach Physical Education in the Secondary School*, Routledge, London

Capel, S, Kelly, L and Whitehead, M (1997) Developing and maintaining an effective learning environment, in *Learning to Teach Physical Education in the Secondary School*, ed S Capel, Routledge, London

Capel, S, Leask, M and Turner, T (1995) *Learning to Teach in the Secondary School*, Routledge, London

Carroll, B (1994) *Assessment in Physical Education: A teacher's guide to the issues*, Falmer, London

CCW (1992) *Physical Education in the National Curriculum*, Curriculum Council for Wales, Cardiff

Christina, R W and Corcos, D M (1988) *Coaches Guide to Teaching Sport Skills*, Human Kinetics, Champaign, IL

Clark, C M and Yinger, R J (1987) Teacher planning, in *Exploring Teachers' Thinking*, ed J Calderhead, Cassell, London

Clay, G (1997) Standards in primary and secondary physical education: OFSTED 1995–6, *British Journal of Physical Education*, **28** (2), pp 5–9

Cohen, L, Manion, L and Morrison, K (1996) *A Guide to Teaching Practice*, Routledge, London

Conway, C (2000) Physical education and the use of ICT, *British Journal of Teaching Physical Education*, **31** (3), pp 12–13

Cooper, P and MacIntyre, D (1996) *Effective Teaching and Learning: Teachers' and students' perspectives*, Open University Press, Buckingham

Cox, M (1999) Using information and communication technologies (ICT) for pupil learning, in *Learning to Teach: A handbook for primary and secondary school teachers*, ed G Nicholls, Kogan Page, London

Cruickshank, D R, Bainer, D L and Metcalf, K (1995) *The Art of Teaching*, McGraw-Hill, New York

Dawney, M (1977) *Interpersonal Judgements in Education*, Harper & Row, London

Dean, J (1996) *Beginning to Teach in the Secondary School*, Open University Press, Buckingham

DES (1978) *Special Educational Needs* (The Warnock Report), HMSO, London

DES (1988) *The New Teacher in School: A survey by HM Inspectors in England and Wales, 1987*, HMSO, London

DES/WO (1989) *Discipline in Schools* (The Elton Report), HMSO, London

DES/WO (1991) *Physical Education for Ages 5–16: Final report of the National Curriculum Physical Education Working Group*, HMSO, London

DFE (1994) *Code of Practice on the Identification and Assessment of Special Educational Needs*, Department for Education, London

DfEE (1997) *Excellence for All Children: Meeting special educational needs*, Department for Education and Employment, London

DfEE (1998a) *Teaching: High standards, high status* (Circular 4/98), Department for Education and Employment, London

DfEE (1998b) *Meeting Special Educational Needs: A programme of action*, Department for Education and Employment, London

DfEE (1998c) National Grid for Learning, http://www.dfee.gov.uk/grid/challenge/index.htm

DfEE (1999a) *Preparing Young People for Adult Life*, DfEE, London

REFERENCES

DfEE (1999b) *Citizenship* (National Curriculum for England), Stationery Office, London

DfEE (2000) National Curriculum for Physical Education, http://www.nc.uk.net/servlets/Subjects?Subject=PE

DNH (1995) *Sport: Raising the game*, Department for National Heritage, London

Evertson, C and Emmer, E (1982) Effective management at the beginning of the school year, *Journal of Educational Psychology*, **74**, pp 485–98

Fernandez-Balboa, J M (1991) Beliefs, interactive thoughts, and actions of physical education student teachers regarding pupil misbehaviours, *Journal of Teaching Physical Education*, **11** (1), pp 59–78

Fisher, C *et al* (1980) Teaching behaviors, academic learning time, and student achievement: an overview, in *Time to Learn*, ed C Denham and A Lieberman, National Institute of Education, Washington, DC

Fisher, R (1995) *Teaching Children to Learn*, Stanley Thornes, Cheltenham

Fitts, P and Posner, M (1967) *Human Performance*, Brooks/Cole, Belmont, CA

Flintoff, A (1998) Sexism and homophobia in physical education: the challenge for teacher education, in *Physical Education: A reader*, ed K Green and K Hardman, Meyer and Meyer, Aachen, Germany

Fontana, D (1985) *Classroom Control: Understanding and guiding classroom behaviour*, British Psychological Society/Methuen, London

Fox, K R (undated) A sporting chance for information technology?, http://www.rice.edn.deakin.edu.au/Archives/DITTE/d55.htm (accessed 7 February 2000)

Foxley, B (1974) *Jean-Jacques Rousseau: Emile*, Dent, London

Gallahue, D (1993) *Developmental Physical Education for Today's Children*, 2nd edn, Brown and Benchmark, Madison, WI

Gardner, J and Walsh, P (2000) ICT and worldmindedness, in *Teaching Values and Citizenship Across the Curriculum: Educating children for the world*, ed R Bailey, Kogan Page, London

Good, T L and Brophy, J E (1991) *Looking at Classrooms*, Harper Collins, New York

Green, K and Scraton, S (1998) Gender, coeducation and secondary physical education: a brief review, in *Physical Education: A reader*, ed K Green and K Hardman, Meyer and Meyer, Aachen, Germany

Hall, A and Leigh, J (2000) *Using the Internet: Physical education*, Pearson, Cambridge

Hall, A and Leigh, J (2001) *ICT in PE: Policy and practice*, Pearson, Cambridge

Hardy, C (1999) Student misbehaviours and teachers' responses in physical education lessons, in *Learning and Teaching in Physical Education*, ed C Hardy and M Mawer, Falmer Press, London

Haring, N G *et al* (1978) *The Fourth R: Research in the classroom*, Charles E Merrill Publ Co, Columbus, OH

Hayes, D (1999) *Planning, Teaching and Class Management: Meeting the standards*, David Fulton, London

Hayes, D (2000) *The Handbook for Newly Qualified Teachers: Meeting the standards in primary and middle schools*, David Fulton, London

Headington, R (2000) *Monitoring, Assessment, Recording, Reporting and Accountability*, David Fulton, London

Hellison, D R and Templin, T J (1991) *A Reflective Approach to Teaching Physical Education*, Human Kinetics, Champaign, IL

Hopper, B, Grey, J and Maude, T (2000) *Teaching Physical Education in the Primary School*, Routledge Falmer, London

ICSSPE (2001) Proceedings of the World Summit on Physical Education, November 3–5, Berlin, 1999, International Council of Sport Science and Physical Education, Berlin

Institute of Youth Sport (2000) *Towards Girl-Friendly Physical Education: The Nike/YST Girls In Sport partnership project (final report)*, IYS, Loughborough

Jacobson, S (1983) *Metacation: Prescription for some ailing educational processes*, Meta Publication, Cupertino, CA

Jowsey, S (1992) *Can I Play Too? Physical education for physically disabled children in mainstream schools*, David Fulton, London

Kagan, S (1988) *Cooperative Learning: Resources for teachers*, Riverside Books, Riverside, CA

Kay, T (1995) *Women and Sport: A review of research*, Sports Council, London

Kemmis, S, Atkin, R and Wright, E (1977) *How Do Pupils Learn?*, Working papers on CAL, Occasional paper 5, University of East Anglia, Centre for Applied Research in Education, Norwich

Kidder, R (1995) *How Good People Make Tough Choices: Resolving the dilemma of ethical living*, William and Morrow, New York

Kounin, J S (1970) *Discipline and Group Management in Classrooms*, Holt, Rinehart and Winston, New York

Kyriacou, C (1991) *Essential Teaching Skills*, Simon and Schuster, Hemel Hempstead

Lambirth, A and Bailey, R P (2000) Promoting a positive learning environment, in *Teaching Physical Education 5–11*, ed R P Bailey and T M Macfadyen, Continuum, London

Langer, E (1989) *Mindfulness*, Perseus, Reading, MA

Laws, C and Fisher, R (1999) Pupils' interpretation of physical education, in *Learning and Teaching in Physical Education*, ed C Hardy and M Mawer, Falmer Press, London

Lee, H D P (tr) (1955) *Plato – The Republic*, Penguin, Harmondsworth

Lee, M (1993) Growing up in sport, in *Coaching Children in Sport: Principles and practice*, ed M Lee, E & F N Spon, London

Macfadyen, T M (2000a) The effective use of teaching styles, in *Teaching Physical Education 5–11*, ed R P Bailey and T M Macfadyen, Continuum, London

Macfadyen, T M (2000b) Creating a safe learning environment in physical education, in *Teaching Physical Education 5–11*, ed R P Bailey and T M Macfadyen, Continuum, London

MacIntosh, P (1957) Games and gymnastics for two nations in one, in *Landmarks in the History of Physical Education*, ed J Dixon *et al*, Routledge & Kegan Paul, London

Mangan, J A (1981) Athleticism: a case study of the evaluation of an educational ideology, in *The Victorian Public School*, ed B Simon and I Bradley, Methuen, London

Marland, M (1975) *The Craft of the Classroom*, Heinemann, London

Martyn, S (1999) Information and communications technology: a learning revolution?, in *The Curriculum for 7–11 Year Olds*, ed J Riley and R Prentice, Paul Chapman Publishing, London

Mawer, M (1995) *The Effective Teaching of Physical Education*, Longman, London

McManus, M (1994) Managing classes, in *Teaching and Learning in the Secondary School*, ed B Moon and A S Mayes, Routledge, London

Meakin, D (1982) Physical education: an agency for moral education, *Journal of Philosophy of Education*, **15** (2), pp 241–54

Metzler, M (1989) A review of research on time in sport pedagogy, *Journal of Teaching in Physical Education*, **8** (2), pp 87–103

Moon, B and Mayes, A S (eds) (1994) *Teaching and Learning in the Secondary School*, Routledge, London

Mortimore, P *et al* (1994) Teacher expectations, in *Teaching and Learning in the Secondary School*, ed B Moon and A S Mayes, Routledge, London

Moyles, J (1988) *Self-Evaluation: A teacher's guide*, NFER, Slough

NCC (1992) *Physical Education: Non-statutory guidance*, National Curriculum Council, York

NCET (1993) *Differentiating the School Curriculum*, Wiltshire Local Education Authority, Wiltshire

Nicholls, G (1995) Helping pupils learn, in *Learning to Teach in the Secondary School: A companion to school experience*, ed S Capel, M Leask and T Turner, Routledge, London

Nicholls, G (1999a) *Learning to Teach: A handbook for primary and secondary school teachers*, Kogan Page, London

Nicholls, G (1999b) Assessment, recording and reporting, in *Learning to Teach: A handbook for primary and secondary school teachers*, ed G Nicholls, Kogan Page, London

O'Connor, J and Seymour, J (1993) *Introducing NLP Neuro-Linguistic Programming*, Harper Collins, London

Office of Her Majesty's Chief Inspector (OHMCI) (1998) *Standards and Quality in Primary Schools: Good practice in physical education and sport*, HMSO, London

OFSTED (1993) *The New Teacher in School*, OFSTED, London

OFSTED (1994) *Primary Matters: A discussion on teaching and learning in primary schools*, Office for Standards in Education, London

Parry, J (1998) The justification for physical education, in *Physical Education: A reader*, ed K Green and K Hardman, Meyer and Meyer, Aachen, Germany

Perrott, E (1982) *Effective Teaching: A practical guide to improving your teaching*, Longman, London

Pik, R (1981) Confrontation situations and teacher-support systems, in *Problem Behaviour in the Secondary School*, ed B Gillham, Croom Helm, London

Piotrowski, S (2000), Assessment, recording and reporting, in *Teaching Physical Education 5–11*, ed R P Bailey and T M Macfadyen, Continuum, London

Placek, J H (1983) Conceptions of success in teaching: busy, happy and good, in *Teaching in Physical Education*, ed T J Templin and J Olson, Human Kinetics, Champaign, IL

Pollard, A and Tann, S (1993) *Reflective Teaching in the Primary School*, 2nd edn, Cassell, London

Pollock, B J and Lee, T D (1992) Effects of model's kill level on observational motor learning, *Research Quarterly for Exercise and Sport*, **63** (1), pp 2–29

Pye, J (1988) *Invisible Children*, Oxford University Press, Oxford

QCA/DfEE (1998) *Education for Citizenship and the Teaching of Democracy in Schools: Final report of the Advisory Group on Citizenship* (The Crick Report), Qualifications and Curriculum Authority, London

Rink, J E (1993) *Teaching Physical Education for Learning*, Mosby, St Louis, MO

Rink, J E (1999) Instruction from a learning perspective, in *Learning and Teaching in Physical Education*, ed C Hardy and M Mawer, Falmer Press, London

Ripley, K, Daines, B and Barrett, J (1997) *Dyspraxia: A guide for teachers and parents*, David Fulton, London

Robertson, C (1999) Early intervention: the education of young children with developmental co-ordination disorder (DCD), in *Young Children Learning*, ed T David, Paul Chapman Publishing, London

Robertson, J (1989) *Effective Classroom Control*, Hodder and Stoughton, London

Romance, T J, Weiss, M R and Bockoven, J (1986) A program to promote moral development through elementary school physical education, *Journal of Teaching in Physical Education*, **5**, pp 126–36

Ross, A (1978) The lecture theatre is a world of entertainment, *Times Educational Supplement*, 23 June

Rowe, F (1997) A ten step guide to the effective use of demonstration in physical education, *Primary PE Focus*, Spring edition, p 23

Saunders, M (1979) *Class Control and Behaviour Problems: A guide for teachers*, McGraw-Hill, Maidenhead

SCAA (1996) *The National Forum for Values Education and the Community*, SCAA, London

Scraton, S (1993) Equality, coeducation and physical education in the secondary school, in *Equality, Education and Physical Education*, ed J Evans, Falmer Press, London

SEAC (1992) *Teacher Assessment at Key Stage 3*, Schools Examination and Assessment Council, London

Shields, D L and Bredemeier, B J (1995) *Character Development and Physical Education*, Human Kinetics, Champaign, IL

Siedentop, D (1991) *Developing Teaching Skills in Physical Education*, Mayfield, Mountain View, CA

Silverman, S (1991) Research on teaching in physical education, *Research Quarterly for Exercise and Sport*, **62** (4), pp 352–64

Sotto, E (1994) *When Teaching Becomes Learning: A theory of practice of teaching*, Cassell, London

Spackman, L (1998) Assessment and recording in physical education, *British Journal of Physical Education*, **29** (4), pp 6–9

Stevenson, L (1975) Socialization effects of participation in sport: a critical review of the research, *Research Quarterly*, **46**, pp 287–301

Sugden, D and Wright, H (1996) Curricular entitlement and implementation for all pupils, in *New Directions in Physical Education: Change and innovation*, ed N Armstrong, Cassell, London

Talbot, M (1996) Gender and National Curriculum physical education, *British Journal of Physical Education*, **27** (1), pp 5–7

Talbot, M (1999) The case for physical education, Paper presented at the World Summit on Physical Education, Berlin, November

Tattum, D (1982) *Disruptive Pupils in School and Units*, Wiley, London

Taylor, P H (1970) *How Teachers Plan Their Courses*, National Foundation for Educational Research, Slough

TTA (2000a) *Career Entry Profile*, Teacher Training Agency, London

TTA (2000b) Using information and communications technology to meet teaching objectives in secondary physical education (ITT exemplification materials), http://www.canteach.gov.uk/info/itt/supporting/ict-exemp.htm

UNESCO (1994) *The Salamanca Statement and Framework for Action*, UNESCO, London

Vickerman, P (1997) Knowing your pupils and planning for different needs, in *Learning to Teach Physical Education in the Secondary School*, ed S Capel, Routledge, London

Wetton, P (1988) *Physical Education in the Nursery and Infant School*, Croom Helm, London

Williams, A (1989) The place of physical education in primary education, in *Issues in Physical Education for the Primary Years*, ed A Williams, Falmer Press, London

Williams, A (1996a) *Teaching Physical Education: A guide for mentors and students*, David Fulton, London

Williams, A (1996b) Physical education at Key Stage 2, in *New Directions in Physical Education: Change and innovation*, ed N Armstrong, Cassell, London

Wragg, E C (ed) (1984) *Classroom Teaching Skills*, Croom Helm, London

Wragg, E C (1993) *Primary Teaching Skills*, Routledge, London

Wragg, E C and Wood, E K (1984a) Teachers' first encounters with their classes, in *Classroom Teaching Skills*, ed E C Wragg, Croom Helm, London

Wragg, E C and Wood, E K (1984b) Pupil appraisals of teaching, in *Classroom Teaching Skills*, ed E C Wragg, Croom Helm, London

Wright, H and Sugden, D (1999) *Physical Education for All: Developing physical education in the curriculum for pupils with special educational needs*, David Fulton, London

Wright, J (1992) Gymnastics in the National Curriculum, *New Directions in Physical Education*, vol 2, ed N Armstrong, Human Kinetics, Champaign, IL

Wright, L (1987) Physical education and moral development, *Journal of Philosophy of Education*, **21** (4), pp 93–102

Index